FOREVER
IS SHORTER

THAN IT
USED TO BE

ALMA
ALEXANDER

ISBN: 978-1-63632-034-2

BOOK VIEW CAFE

Book View Café
304 S. Jones Blvd, Suite 2906
Las Vegas, NV89107

FOREVER
IS SHORTER
THAN IT
USED TO BE

Finding

(But It Took Years,

And a Miracle or Two)

I suppose it all began when… but before that, there was… no, two steps back from that we…

This is a story that had no real beginning. It will never really have an end. It existed—it exists—it was always there, and it will never be over.

But now, lost as I am in the interstices of time as the story changed around me in painful ways, I can't help feeling around for memories, for clues. I keep coming back to the metaphor of a jigsaw puzzle that is my life, and trying very hard to put together the pieces that match in pattern or in shade—except that now there is a piece missing, a piece that will always be missing, a piece I will never have again, and all I am left with of the original image is that thing printed on the lid of the puzzle box, still perfect, but now just a memory and something that I will never again be able to recreate or hold in my hand.

I met a man. He met me. We met each other. We connected. We married. We loved.

And now he is gone.

This book is largely about him and how I lost him—a journey into the darkest heart of grief—but, like I said just now, it all started before that. It started nearly a quarter of a century ago. And what is a story about him, and about loss, begins as a story about us, about finding miracles, about love, about belonging. Because if you don't know about that, then you will never understand just what it is that has been lost.

At the time we connected, Internet-borne relationships were rare enough (no "swiping right" and dating apps back then). It was largely his idea that we write a book about it—alternating chapters between him and me—but because he quickly came to the conclusion, as he told me, that he "used to think that he was a writer before he met me", the thing kind of devolved wholly to me—although he DID contribute a little, right at the beginning of it all—and the book we tentatively called "Cyberdance", as a descriptor of what transpired between us, kept on getting pushed into the archives and onto back burners as I wrote and published (many) other books. Certainly nobody has ever seen any of that material except him and me... until now. Because, well, let's say that if we can't really pin down the beginning of this story... let's start it here. With material that I originally wrote back in 2003. Let me tell you our story, from that beginning.

☙

From "Cyberdance"

CHAPTER 1: OPENING THE CYBERDOOR
ALMA

"LIFE IS A CIRCLE," I said, "where do we start?"

An arm's length away, my husband turned to chuckle at me. "You do know I have the whole of our early correspondence saved...? That seems like a good place to find a beginning."

"You'd better email it to me," I said, without thinking.

It struck both of us at the same time, and we turned to grin at one another. It was a strange, strange, strange world. We had met with the odds against us—the cyberworld tends to put new meanings on needles in haystacks in certain contexts—and at a distance which, a few short years ago, would probably have meant that we would never have known of each other's existence. Email changed all that, with instantaneous communication across the miles. But so used had we, and millions like us, become to the magic of transferring thoughts and data in the electronic medium that it seemed like the only sensible thing to do was for him to transfer the files of our early correspondence from his computer to mine via an email.

We were sitting at practically the same desk, our computers (when we married many things became "ours" but computers remained largely His and Hers) barely four feet apart, and yet the information which he had and I required was about to be entrusted into an email which would leave his computer terminal, race off into HIS phone line, probably get bounced through London, Atlanta, Seattle, Reykjavik, Outer Mongolia, and Timbuctoo via a couple of different satellites, find itself routed back into Florida, zip into MY phone line, and announce its presence on my screen with a ping less than a minute later.

I found myself remembering one of those Reader's Digest "I am John's finger" type articles, or something similar, where I had encountered a particular passage which now came to haunt me: "The fingertip touches a hotplate; the nerve endings react with 'Yikes, that's hot, it hurts'. The message races along the nerves in the arm, straight into the relevant section of the brain. The brain responds with, 'Well, move away, then!' The messages races *back* along the same route, and the hand responds by snatching the fingertip away from the offensive area. The whole thing takes a fraction of a second."

Could the Internet really be a huge living thing, like the eponymous John's body, and all of us within it, living our little lives, only its synapses and sinews? Sometimes it's almost tempting to think so; certainly the beast behaves as though it had a mind of its own, stalling or working at lightning speeds at its own pace and for no discernible reason. Things called "servers" bounce one's messages and don't have to offer any explanation other than that they are mysteriously "busy". Bad phone lines offer slow connections. Frustration, wrath and resignation follow each other in quick succession. But us synapses and sinews are wired into the system by now. Addicted, us? We can all quit, really, any time. Just as soon as we answer this last email…

The world was a much smaller place for me only a few short years ago. It was true that I had seen a great deal more of it than most of my contemporaries—but that was through the vagaries of life and being part of a family where a changing job of the breadwinner required the entire family to shift to a new place every few years.

I was born in what used to be Yugoslavia before its disintegration. In the aftermath of that disintegration, my father and mother now come from "different countries", the fractured remnants of that nation. I am very definitely the fruit of a mixed marriage between a scion of a Herzegovina (as in Bosnia and Herzegovina, which used to be the actual name of the 'country' the world has since learned to know as Bosnia) family of Muslim faith and Serb ethnic origin, and the older daughter of a schoolteacher from Vojvodina, the far north of Serbia. Both families cast a long shadow, way back to a medieval battle of three centuries ago—the name of that ill-fated battlefield would become all too familiar within my own lifetime. My mother's family finally migrated from Kosovo to Vojvodina in the mid-1600's. My father's ancestor fought at the Battle of Kosovo back in 1389, survived to hobble home with a permanently crippled leg (which gave rise to our surname—Hromic—in my language, "hrom" means "he who limps" so the surname is quite literally "son of the gimp"), and was rewarded with a dukedom for his trouble. The title, of course, is long lost in the weight of history that had been piled onto this small patch of fractious, history-heavy, and beloved land; but, at least in theory, I am still a Duchess with a coat of arms.

When my father got his first United Nations assignment, in Zambia, I was barely ten years old. The sojourn outside Yugoslavia was supposed to last all of two years or so. It turned into twenty, with Zambia being replaced with Swaziland and then South Africa. I left South Africa thirteen years after we had moved there, when the security situation started meaning a virtual curfew and house arrest for a single white female with no escort and no gun, and moved to New Zealand—far enough from trouble and strife for it to be truly the Other Side of the Fence and where, thus, the grass was definitely greener.

I arrived in Auckland in April 1994, and spent the next couple of years getting acclimatised. I lurched into a disastrous relationship, and, when that failed, into one that promised to be everything that I had ever dreamed of. John loved his country, and showed me more of New Zealand in the space of the eleven months which I shared with him than most born–and–bred Kiwis (as the locals referred to themselves) see in a lifetime. From the breathtaking fjords and the imposing Southern Alps in the South Island, to the bubbling sulphurous mud and the geysers of Rotorua in the North, I saw it all, and my horizons were opened by it. But a far greater gift that John left me crystallised one evening at his place, in front of a glowing computer screen.

"You mean I can really talk to *anybody*?" I asked, awed at what I just understood email to mean. "Right now? Right here?"

"Sure," he said, with a grin. "Want to try it?"

I knew only one email address then—a fact that leaves me slightly bemused now—and I typed up an awkward message to an ex–lecturer and friend back at the University of Cape Town where I had got my postgraduate degree. I pressed *send*. The email disappeared.

I received no reply, and I forgot all about it for a short while. And then a local Internet Service Provider, or ISP, announced that they were introducing a flat rate account instead of the usual hourly rate which had prevailed up until then and which, if I had taken it up at the time, would have bankrupted me very quickly. It suddenly became a viable option for me to acquire my own

Internet account. So, tentatively, I signed up.

My first email was to John: "Just testing. If you don't get this message, let me know."

Little did I know that I was establishing a pattern. In a few short months I would have an international smart–aleck reputation that I would never quite shed again.

Events moved on, and just as John and I parted company—painfully—I was discovering the strange new world of the cyberpeople. A good friend with a bit more Internet experience had told me about a phenomenon called Usenet—a seemingly inexhaustible supply of discussion groups on every topic under the sun. Devotees of Britney Spears, Doctor Who, every blessed version of Star Trek that ever came out, Jane Austen, quilt making, geology, organic gardening, frogs, politics, madrigals, Alfred Hitchcock, fictional taverns and distant planets and your back yard, the kitchen sink and the human genome—all of them could find a home on Usenet where people like them, interested in the same thing, would gather and discuss the matter at hand. Usenet groups, to a greater or lesser extent, evolved into enclaves or cliques. Anywhere you went you would be able to discern, with a bit of time and effort, distinct circles of—if not friends, exactly—people whose opinions gibed with one another's to the extent that they would be a support to each other. The quarrels that blew up in these discussion groups could be incredibly virulent given the often largely irrelevant–to–the–world–at–large topic under discussion; it was with reason that these became known as flame wars, with certain people developing well deserved reputations for being able to singe the hair off your eyebrows with a few well–chosen and precisely aimed fiery phrases. (There was even a Usenet group—alt.flame—where practitioners of this "art" went to hone their skills…)

But Usenet groups—some of them, the best of them, perhaps—also evolved into what began to resemble dysfunctional families. Long–standing regulars with established viewpoints and well–known hot buttons would be the fixtures around which more itinerant groups fluttered, formed, re–formed, disintegrated, shifted and danced. A writer by interest and, for some time now, profession, I gravitated to a writing newsgroup—and found a place called misc.writing.

I first meandered in there sometime in April 1996, drawn just as much by the "writing" aspect of it as by the existence of something called "misc.writingville", or MWV, which was a virtual community, an imaginary village, peopled by the denizens of the group. Some time later the misc.writing group, or MW, would produce T–shirts emblazoned with the logo of Kate's Bar and Grill, a watering hole on the corner of the streets of Hope and Despair in the 'Ville. It was all in our heads, of course—the life of the place rested in the creative minds of the people who 'lived' there, and there would be long, involved, interactive exchanges where people slipped into persona and wrote what was only nominally fiction. The 'fiction' almost always centered on current events, on–group or off–group in the larger world, and were frequently cutting satires on those events. This was a writer's playground, and words made *wonderful* toys.

I lurked for a while—that is to say, I hung back and observed the messages or posts that came up on my screen when I called up the group, learning the personalities and the lay of the land. But not too long. My first MWV post was a plaintive, "What's a girl got to do to get a cup of coffee around here?" In the spirit of the fantasy game we were playing, a salt–of–the–earth character known by all and sundry as the Last Real Marlborough Man posted a near immediate response to my post saying, "It mayn't be much, but what I got is yours to share." It didn't take much more than that to make me lose my heart to this strange place in the never–never land of the cyberworld, and start making fast friends there.

Misc.writing was a newsgroup chartered for the discussion of writing, in all its shapes and forms. There were people there who take the stance that *everything* is about writing, and therefore no topic of discussion is ever really forbidden or censured in that group. The topics do include those closely related to the craft of writing—and there are long threads of linked messages involving formatting of manuscripts for submission to publishers, marketing tips, characterisation, dialogue advice, answers to questions about genre, grammar, and length of chapters. They also include sheep (for which the group had a definite penchant), chocolate, pun cascades (where I am an inveterate repeat offender) and politics of all persuasions.

About a year after I got there, MW threw out one of its long–standing controversies when one of its better–known denizens wrote a fiery, impassioned post on the subject of police brutality. The context was a particular case where a man, committed to some sort of a psychiatric facility, decided to check himself out, and emerged from the entrance to the building (after some minor fracas inside) clutching what had been described as 'a knife'. The police, who had been called, were waiting outside; they called to the man to drop his weapon, he not only ignored them but started towards them... and they shot him. In the aftermath, the knife in question was shown to be a harmless and quite blunt butterknife.

The Butterknife Debate ran hot, and ran long. It was something where opinions were put forward and defended, and one learned, perforce, many things about one's on–line friends which one may not have quite known before. It was something that happened in the United States, far from my beaten path, but I too had an opinion. Naturally. When I expressed it, I found myself in skirmishes with several people on the group. One of these turned into an email correspondence, initially on the Butterknife Debate itself. In a message from the archives dated 10 May 1997 a man by the name of Deck Deckert and I finally "agreed to differ" on this subject. [*AA(comment)*]: although we both maintained that the other 'lost', ever after. As a reminder, we finally framed a butterknife and hung it in our kitchen. It was an icon of our relationship and a defuser of all fights—if things ever got heated, one or the other of us would point to the framed butterknife, and the fight was over...] I said something along the lines of, "...and I look forward to more one–liner deckisms (nobody does those posts quite the way you do) in misc.writing." The one–liners, achingly precise and often monosyllabic replies that showed up many a pompous windbag for being just that, had already earned Deck a place in the English language (at least within the newsgroup, that is) as such rejoinders became known as being "deckish".

The famous deckisms, however, remained in the group. Outside the group, and leaving in our wake the Butterknife Controversy, Deck and I struck up an email correspondence which quickly ranged far and wide, discussing science and science fiction, and skirting other, more important subjects.

On June 9, he wrote, "I'm a freelance writer and ex–newsman. The only science in my training is my BA in psychology, and I won't tell you how long ago I got that."

"Why not?" I asked in the return message.

"Ah, you're cruel," he replied. "I got my BA in 1959."

"NOW I will be cruel," I said. "I wasn't *born* until the middle of 1963..."

One or two messages later he grumbled darkly that everyone he met in cyberspace seemed to be 'Melrose Place' young, "... and all of the interesting *women* I meet in cyberspace are too young, attached, or live in different countries or continents. Or all three."

He then had the grace to ask how he could get my autobiography, "Houses in Africa", published only a few months earlier in New Zealand. So, he was older than me (we discovered by just how much in the space of the next email or two—28 years. And I managed to work somewhere in there that I, um, *liked* my men older than me). So what? He was courteous, he was kind, he was full of dryly humorous wit. All of his, despite his misguided approach to the facts of the Butterknife Incident (he maintains, to this day, that the same is true of me), made this man someone I would be proud to call my friend.

So I did. For some time, despite the initial careful probes, it went no further than a fun correspondence. But we managed to sprinkle our emails with snatches of information about one another. We established that he was a lark and I was an owl, in other words, that I would be quite happy staying up until dawn and he preferred simply getting up when the sun rose. He wasn't a poetry reader, but he asked for one of mine and I sent it; and he liked it. I suppose he learned far more about me from that poem than I cared to think about. However, finally, he said, "you have told me little about yourself. Is everything in the book? [*"Houses in Africa, which he had ordered*] Must I wait for the book? Hmmmmm?"

And I replied, "Hmmmmm. <g> The book's just a part of it, what do you want to know? I was born in a country which no longer exists and then spent years tumbling around the planet like the professional tumbleweed that I am, following my shadow. I came to New Zealand alone, in April 94, not knowing a soul in this place. Within the last three years I managed to live a lifetime. I could tell you about it but it's probably more than you wanted to know. I feel rather like I've put on spiked armour during this time—except that the spikes are all pointing inwards, and the closer the armour fits the deeper the spikes go until one day they pierce into the heart of me. Oh dear, caught me at the wrong time… I do have my little black holes… Backtracking rapidly. I am a grey–haired redhead, by which I mean that I went grey from my natural golden chestnut shade when I was 17 years old and have been stubbornly dyeing my hair ever since because I refuse to go grey before I am forty. (In fact, my dad once called me a professional nut, with my chestnut hair and hazel eyes). Let's see, what else did you want to know? I've got a birthday coming up in two weeks, I'm a microbiologist with a master's degree who is working as a text–book editor, I love coffee and chocolate, I don't like asparagus and olives, and I'm allergic to fish and wasps and the occasional medicine. Mosquitoes love me. And damn it, I don't know much about you either, aside from the fact that you have spinning crises in midair while skydiving, land on unsuspecting melons while parachuting, used to have a pilot's licence, and occasionally have to be bailed out of computer catastrophes by your son <g>. Oh, and that you're one of the finest writers in MW—although I can't always agree with your point of view, I am always struck anew by your ability to distil into clarity. All I do, in between the occasional serious post, is hone my reputation for punnery and wordplay. As they say in tennis doubles, 'yours'. How about a potted bio?"

The bio came back the next day.

"Deck is an idealist, a cynic, shy, socially inept, a lousy businessman, a procrastinator, a writer, a reader, a sceptic, a seeker, a hater of bigotry, a sensualist, a lover, a sentimentalist, a near–pacifist, a non–athlete who used to bike and hike, a skydiver for reasons still beyond understanding, a father, a fat man with brown hair and white beard becoming slimmer after embracing vegetarianism, a man fascinated by UFOs, ghosts and psychic abilities, a man awed by the wonders of the infinity of the wonders around him—and a man who is chagrined that a most interesting woman he recently met lives a half world away, and is just a youngster about to celebrate the fifth anniversary of her 29th birthday. Sigh."

I took it point by point in my reply, mostly saying "me too".

When I responded "Oh?" to his "a sensualist and a lover" self–characterisations, he wrote back, "I think that a bout of love–making should last at least an hour, and the preliminaries are usually more fun than the main event <g> I enjoy good wine, good food, good music, a good sunset, a babbling brook and a walk through autumn leaves."

I could not help it. I wrote back, half–jokingly and half in earnest, "Oh, *God*, Deck, will you marry me?"

CHAPTER 2: FOREVER AUTUMN
DECK

ALMA AND I WERE STROLLING through our local Barnes & Noble a few months after we were married, holding hands, as usual. I wrapped my arm around her waist and stopped to give her a brief kiss, as usual.

"Get a room!" a voice said peremptorily.

We looked up, expecting to see a friend. Instead, we saw a store official, an imposing woman in her 40s, a smile on her face that I thought stern and forced but which Alma thought merely smug. I didn't recognize her, but I have no particular facility with names and faces (a shameful failing for a writer), and thought she was probably one of my past students. I smiled and looked at her inquiringly, expecting some further jocular comment.

At this she faltered a bit and said lamely, "And in front of the wedding section too."

We looked to our right at the rows and rows of books on bridal gowns, wedding etiquette, and floral arrangements, and best man speeches. Alma smiled and displayed her engagement ring and wedding band. "Been there, done that," she said sweetly.

Now clearly flustered, the woman began backpedaling in earnest. "Unh, second honeymoon, right?"

"No, the first," Alma said, and the woman retreated in complete confusion.

I kept an eye out for her as we wandered through the store, hoping to make her uncomfortable with another public display of affection, but she never came close to us again.

We immediately labeled the incident: Mr. & Mrs. Dorky Do Barnes & Noble. It was only the first in the series. "Mr. & Mrs. Dorky" have been doing everything from the movie house to the local supermarket.

I can't claim any prescience about the changes that cyberspace in general and the Internet in particular would make in my life.

Posting messages in discussion groups and developing email relationships with people all over the world was just a hobby. It kept me off the streets and away from the mindlessness of TV. I had no idea it would lead me to a new life as Mr. Dorky.

In the beginning, Alma was just another email friend I scarcely knew. But her first emails were filled with good humor and her intelligence shone through in everything she said. I've always been a sucker for smart women. And it is heady stuff when a woman scarcely more than half your age asks if you'll marry her.

Of course, I knew that Alma was joking when she made her proposal. At least I had assumed she was–I didn't know until I read her first draft of this book that she had been "half in earnest." But I preened a bit anyhow. Not to the point of even mentioning it to my friends, you understand, I didn't want to look like the classic old fool.

The age gap is a peculiar thing. Alma and I have moved past it now and it has no meaning in our daily lives. But it wasn't always so. It was a rock in the middle of the dance floor as we began our cyberdance. I stumbled clumsily around it in our early correspondence, always fearful of coming across as a Dirty Old Man. I routinely screened out the sexually-tinged jokes that I sent on to a score of other Internet friends, for example, and generally avoided any suggestion that I saw her as more than a platonic friend.

Until I met Alma, I consciously avoided ever mentioning my age in email or discussion group postings. Cyberspace was, and mostly still is, a world of the young—teens, 20-somethings, 30-somethings—and I felt, and still do, that in most contexts my contribution would be subtly discounted if my age were known. The hippies of the Sixties may have abandoned the mantra 'Don't trust anyone over 30' as they themselves aged, but it is still alive and well in most of cyberspace, even if not so bluntly stated.

I was a Depression baby, born in Connecticut in 1935 and raised on another mantra that reflected the desperation of the times: Waste not, want not. Use it up, wear it out, make it do, or do without. It made me frugal and helped shape my disinterest in 'things,' unnecessary material goods. A friend, born in the same era, has always said he doesn't 'need' anything more than could fit in the footlocker he had as a young marine. He's not quite fanatical about it and lives in a modest but comfortable home. But there are amazingly few possessions scattered about that home, although he has a comfortable income. I understand where he is coming from, although my home is cluttered with some things... mainly thousands of books.

I was a 'blue baby' and the doctor gave my mother some disastrous advice: feed him well. She did. I was a fat baby who grew into a fat child and suffered the fate of most fat children in America. I became the butt of jokes and was relentlessly teased. I was too shy to adopt the defensive strategy of many fat kids, becoming the class clown. Football wasn't much of a sport in those days so I couldn't put my bulk to work on the athletic field to gain some positive attention. Wouldn't have worked anyhow as I was, and am, about as athletic as a stuffed bear.

My last year in high school I begged my family doctor for some help in losing weight. He put me on bennies. I began dropping two pounds a week, and by the time I graduated I was a slightly pudgy but otherwise normal kid. I started college as a freshman, not 'the fat kid.' It was glorious.

It also didn't last long. By my sophomore year at the University of Connecticut I was putting on weight again, and by the time I graduated, I was fat enough that the army decided my weight, coupled with an old knee injury, made me unfit for service.

I graduated with a BA in psychology in 1959. One needs advanced degrees to go anywhere in the field of psychology and I put aside my useless BA and drifted into newspapering. By the time Alma was born, I was working for the Palm Beach Times. She was wearing diapers while I was putting out the Kennedy assassination edition, and anticipating making my mark in the world of journalism. I never did, mostly because I lacked the single-minded drive that lies behind most success stories.

While Alma was growing up in Yugoslavia and Africa, I was working for a succession of Florida newspapers—Orlando Sentinel, Palm Beach Times, Lakeland Ledger, Pompano Sun-Sentinel, Miami Herald, and the Miami News and acquired a wife and a family. When my first wife and I separated and then divorced, the older kids were teenagers nearly ready to start lives of their own. Our youngest son was only seven and we agreed that he would live with me most of the time, visiting her on weekends.

I left the Miami News, moved up the Florida coast to Palm City, and began freelancing in the hopes of making a living without leaving my boy to be raised by a succession of babysitters and day care workers.

Shortly after that, I discovered computers and computer bulletin boards and began my cyberspace odyssey.

Before the Internet exploded into public awareness in the late 80s, there were computer bulletin boards. A bulletin board, nearly always referred to as a BBS, standing for Bulletin Board System, was simply a computer. Sometimes, rather often in fact, it was owned by a teenager and sat in the corner of his bedroom under a poster of a rock star or Captain Kirk. I doubt if anyone knows exactly how many there really were, but there were thousands of them.

Anyone with a computer of his own could phone up the BBS computer and see what was stored there. The initial trick was to find it in the first place. To the world at large, they were invisible. The usual first step was to call up some computer store, or computer club, and ask for the name and phone number of any BBS's in the area.

When you finally made a connection, your computer screen would fill with information, nearly always just text. It was a lot easier to display words than pictures. What you got depended on the particular BBS you called. It might be a tale about a neat new game the sysop (the guy who owned or ran the place) had discovered or a lament about a lost love. There would most likely be a place where you could post a message and respond to messages posted by others, everything from politics to scurrilous attacks on other posters.

The BBS era lasted only a few years. It began in the late 70s, grew amazingly fast, and then died a few years later when the Internet exploded into the public consciousness in the mid and late 80s. For most of us who took part in it, the memories are as bittersweet as those of a first love. There was an air of magic, mystery, and innocence about it that was lost when big business interests got involved, first with giant commercial bulletin boards like AOL and then the Internet, with its millions of World Wide Web sites devoted to selling, selling, selling.

Already I've forgotten too many details, including the names of some people who were important to me at the time. And remember, we're talking about a period that ended a little over a decade ago. When I asked a couple of friends to jog my memory about our personal BBS world on the Treasure Coast of Florida, they both noted with some chagrin that they too have already forgotten too much of it.

"It's amazing how quickly the Internet overran that whole era, and how quickly the details have evaporated from memory," said my friend Rob. Rob ran a BBS called Simple Mind on the Treasure Coast of Florida. (Every inch of Florida, it seems, has to have its own special name: Gold Coast, Space Coast, etc. The Treasure Coast is the area lying roughly between West Palm Beach and Cape Canaveral).

Rob's board had only one telephone line and thus only one person at a time could connect with it. This precluded any form of 'chat,' that is, people talking (typing) to each other on their computers at the same time. On one-line boards, exchanges were limited to leaving messages that a later caller could respond to.

Multi-line boards did offer chat potential, however, and one

Treasure Coast board, Info-Power, had 20 lines. Customers could, and frequently did, get involved in 20-way chats. Unfortunately, the art of conversation was not particularly advanced by the advent of computer chat on bulletin boards—more later on the Internet.

During one 20-way chat, I told the others that I had just analyzed the 'conversation' to that point and discovered that it consisted of "42 percent hellos and goodbyes, 23 percent bad jokes, 18 percent questions about who was going with who, and 17 percent talk about the weather." I was only half joking.

While there were thousands of bulletin boards scattered across the country, and the world, the BBS world was actually a small one, or a series of small worlds. The bulletin boards were local and if you didn't know the other people who called in the beginning—they were likely to use handles such as Calgirl, Bambamjr, Stormy, Islegal, Geobear, Fuzzy, Alpha, and Hushpuppy you soon discovered who they really were and where they lived, usually only a few miles from you.

Thus small communities grew up around the more popular boards. The people on Info-Power, the board of 20 lines, had frequent parties and picnics. Romances were frequent, and at least one led to a wedding that took place online. A number of the BBS regulars gathered in the living room of the sysop along with the couple and the notary who would be officiating at the wedding ceremony. I sat at a computer and typed in a running account of the wedding ceremony for people online, which included the groom's family in Wisconsin. When they were pronounced husband and wife, the congratulations from all the online observers scrolled rapidly across the screen.

The experience of watching a romance begin in cyberspace was fascinating, but I had no clairvoyant glimpses of my own future.

I drifted away from the BBS world myself, feeling vaguely guilty about it, when I got my first Internet connection and discovered Usenet, the collection of scores of thousands of discussion groups that are available on the Internet. I never looked back.

Someone, I don't remember who, told me how to locate a discussion group called misc.writing. Sometime about the mid-90s I began lurking.

I had already discovered that each newsgroup has its own personality, its own culture. Some were cantankerous, filled with snarling people. Some were rigidly orthodox, with no deviation from the main focus of the group allowed. The level of discussion ranged from scholarly to first grade playground.

Misc.writing was filled with intelligent people chatting, and chattering, about everything from sheep to politics with mostly wry good humor. There were periodic discussions on whether there was enough discussion of writing in this writing group. Newcomers—it was almost always a newcomer—would survey the 200 to 300 messages posted a day and demand to know why nobody was sticking to the subject of writing. Such messages were met with sighs, snarls, or laughs and the explanation that misc.writing was most closely akin to a coffee house, a place where writers could relax, swap a few jokes, exchange writing and marketing tips, and generally chat with friends. At its very best, not often of course, it resembled the Algonquin Club frequented by Dorothy Parker and other luminaries in the 20s.

I was charmed. Misc.writing became my first stop when roaming in cyberspace, and I moved from lurking to occasional participation.

I don't know when I first noticed one of Alma's posts. That seems a bit disgraceful now, but it's the simple truth. I was vaguely aware that she liked to pun and often initiated or joined in pun cascades, a series of messages from posters each trying to top the other's puns. All writers love one form or another of word play, but puns were never my specialty or interest. My writing heroes tend to be terse and often caustic, and the quick sharp rejoinder, for good or ill, became my trademark in misc.writing, as elsewhere.

I became aware of Alma as something other than a punaholic in the infamous Butterknife Incident that she has already alluded to. As a newsman I'd been aware of far too many occasions when the police overreacted and hurt or killed people and how rarely they are ever called to account for their errors, miscalculations, and sometimes gross incompetence. I am not, in short, likely to automatically assume that the police are always right. Alma has the more traditional attitude that always, or at least nearly always, gives the police the benefit of the doubt. We batted this proposition around in misc.writing messages and in private email until we agreed to disagree.

That was our first disagreement about life, the universe and everything, but it was hardly our last, which, I think, was about an hour ago. [*AA: DISAGREEMENT. We squabbled. Most couples do. But we only had three serious FIGHTS in twenty years of marriage. That, I think, is a good track record and worth recording...*]

I established my age as soon as it was clear that we would become cyberfriends. While I have no compunctions about hiding my age in group settings like misc.writing, I couldn't do the same in a one-on-one email relationship with someone who I thought, even then, might be significant in my life.

Early on I invited her for a visit, at the time telling myself it would be avuncular. Acknowledging our conflicting lark and owl tendencies, I put it like this: "Come visit me and you can stay up to dawn and I'll get up at dawn. We can enjoy the early morning silence together watching the sun rise over the Atlantic Ocean, or the Everglades."

"Aren't there alligators in them thar swamps?" she asked in what she thought was an American Southern accent. "Let's go to the Keys instead."

"It's a deal," I replied cheerfully. "Despite the best efforts of the politicians and developers to destroy the Keys, they remain, at least for now, a place of extraordinary beauty. And I'd do my best to take you up to see them from the air. My pilot's license is inactive but I could probably get a friend to take us up. The colors are indescribable—a dozen shades of green on land, a hundred shades of blue and green in the water. A brilliant blue sky and clouds as white and frilly as a wedding gown. Boats drawing graceful lines in the water. And a horizon that extends forever."

It was quite some time before we finally got to the Keys.

Our email conversation roamed back and forth across our lives. I spoke of some of my skydiving misfortunes and she gibed, "I can't figure out if God loves you too little or too much, Deck."

"God didn't give me the grace to be a skydiver," I retorted, "so She may have been taunting me. <g> My logbook looks like the shooting script for the Perils of Pauline—tree landings, three broken legs, a torn-up knee (a line wrapped around it while the canopy was trying to inflate and it acted like a garrote), ripped canopy, lost ripcords, lost helmet, smashed altimeter, a swamp landing, and a landing on a watermelon."

She found the last humiliating incident far too funny.

She countered my skydiving stories with accounts of skiing in the Canadian Rockies one Christmas when it was below zero, and swimming with the dolphins in the South Pacific.

We spoke of our school days and hometowns. I was fascinated by her life in what to me were exotic locations—Yugoslavia, South Africa, Zambia, Swaziland, and New Zealand. When I discovered that she had written a book about growing up in Africa, I immediately asked to buy a copy. When "Houses in Africa" arrived, I read it avidly and discovered Alma is a graceful and lyrical writer and an excellent storyteller. I searched for a picture of her in her book and found one of her holding a lion club. It wasn't a studio style portrait, but it gave me some sense of what she looked like. I found her charming.

It was during these early exchanges that one of our family catchphrases was coined. "You know why they don't send donkeys to school, don't you?" I asked after she gleefully pointed out a grammatical error I'd made.

"No."

"Because nobody likes a smart ass," I said tartly.

As we are both smart asses by nature, that became a much-used refrain.

I may have already been falling in love with her. If not, I'm sure an email she sent me in honor of autumn began tipping me over the edge, echoing as it did so many of the things I felt.

"A few years ago, one October I found myself in London's Hyde Park early one Sunday morning. The place was almost deserted—a few people walking dogs, two swans sleeping by the duck pond, someone bundled in a duffle coat and asleep on a park bench. There were just enough leaves remaining on the deciduous trees to make them flame gold in the young sun streaking through the streamers of morning mist, and against them the firs and pines were full of shadows, dark and brooding. And spread on the ground was a Persian carpet of whispering leaves.

"The ground was damp—not boggy, but soft underfoot, with the merest suspicion that what you were walking on was incipient mud. The leaves were red and gold, tumbled, just stirred by the breeze. The air was cool with the first breath of winter, bright with late autumn sunshine, only the hum of traffic and the murmuring leaves breaking the silence.

"I walked across the lawn, kicking at the leaves like a kid, watching them flutter up and settle down again, and before long I realised that the reason they were getting increasingly blurred in my sight was that my eyes were brimming with tears. Ask me why I was crying and I couldn't tell you—maybe it was something to do with the brightness of the air, and a kaleidoscope of memories, jewel-like in my mind, that were stirred like the leaves at my feet with every step. Maybe I'm just too sentimental for my own good. I don't know. All I can tell you is that I walked out of there, back into the real world, with the feeling of having been to a place that was not of this earth, and not of this time. To this day I remember it vividly, that quiet golden morning, like I've just left it."

I ached to take a walk through autumn with this woman.

CHAPTER 3: WHAT IF…?

ALMA

CHRISTMAS 1995 WAS STILL HAPPY for me and John, a sort of a personal Indian summer. We flew down to the South Island in a two–seater single engine aircraft, which was a glorious and exotic adventure for me, and spent Christmas together in the picturesque resort town of Queenstown, on Lake Wakatipu. The lake was high; the town had had some flooding that season, and in some streets sandbags still held back the inundation (the remnants of the floods lapped at the doorway of a restaurant which advertised "fresh fish daily", which tickled my off–the–wall sense of humor). If I had believed in portents I might have thought the place was almost too painfully beautiful, and I was almost too happy. Neither condition could last. We would leave Queenstown after a few glorious days there, and within a few short months after that John and I ourselves would be history. By Easter of the following year, I was on my own.

❧

THE SOMEWHAT UNEXPECTED RESULT OF this was the sudden urge to spend Christmas of 1996 somewhere else—somewhere far away, as far away from New Zealand and its memories as I could get. The choice fell on the Canadian Rockies, and I found myself spending a week or so in Banff on a skiing holiday. The winter was the coldest they had had for thirty years—or so they kept telling me. I believed it. I was constantly disappearing into equipment shops to acquire an extra pair of gloves or an extra pair of socks to prevent my extremities from freezing on the ski slopes where the temperatures fell to as low as −28° Celsius. It was the first "white Christmas" I had spent in almost thirty years, and I was irrationally delighted with the freezing temperatures and the huge snowbanks. I had come out there to forget, and it had worked; I had given myself a whole new set of things to remember about Christmas.

But the trip had one last gift to offer. Before I would board the plane back to Auckland, in January 1997, I had already arranged something that I was looking forward to with a great deal of excitement. I'd sent out an email into "my" newsgroup, misc. writing, saying that I would be in Vancouver for a few days on my way home from Canada, and would anyone from that general neck of the woods care to meet me for a cup of coffee or something?

Jen Jensen generously transformed the cup of coffee into a delicious dinner at her place, together with another misc.writer, Stephanie Kwok, the maintainer of the newsgroup's webpage. Jen's husband watched in some bemusement as these three women, at least one of whom was a total stranger to the others, chattered as though they had known one another for years. Photos were taken; they would be posted on the Web in short order. Anonymity was a thing of the past. It was the first time I had ever met up with any of the other MW denizens, aside from my friend Maggie back in Auckland who had introduced me to the group in the first place. The experience was wonderful, and was to prove remarkably addictive.

In August 1997 a somewhat larger group of misc.writers gathered in Austin, Texas, at what was to become known as the first "wrevel". Paul Harwood, who coined the term, had typed "revel" in a post he was about to send off to the group, pondered on how *wrong* it looked, and on impulse added a w to the beginning of the word. The misc.writing parties would never be known by any other name from that day forward. The first wrevel was attended by a handful of group "regulars" who were pretty much household names for those of us who had been on–line and on the group for a reasonable length of time. The party spawned all sorts of relics in its wake (misc.writing's own coffee mugs, and several kinds of designer T–shirts produced in the USA but purchased from as far afield as New Zealand and Sweden). It also started a trend, one that made me, out there all the way across the Pacific, very envious—those within reasonable distance of one another began having these "wrevels" as a semi–regular occurrence. I was always too far away to think about attending—the costs would have been astronomical. Some of these wrevels I attended vicariously, as it were, because the wrevellers invested in a phone card and phoned me all the way in New Zealand, which was great. But I wanted more than that—I wanted to be a part of this phenomenon. In person. For real. I had had a taste of the cyberworld translated into reality, and I wanted more.

When the so–called "First International Wrevel" was proposed, to take place in Vancouver on the Easter long weekend of 1998, I impulsively bought tickets to Canada. It was partly the running away thing again. It would be two years at Easter since I picked up the shards of my shattered heart.

I confided my plans in only one person, Stephanie Kwok, whom I had met previously on that brief visit to Vancouver the previous Christmas—and that only because I wanted someone to book my hotel room for the wrevel anonymously since I wanted my presence there to be a surprise. Stephanie crowed in the group about her Secret Guest, and I was promptly re–christened, mocking the spirit of the Internet paranoia still prevalent amongst the general populace when it came to meeting electrons–made–flesh, as a Mystery Ax Murderer Guest.

Two things happened as a result of my decision to go. One of my great Internet friends, Ari Nordstrom from Sweden, decided to come along too if I was going to be there. And, in email, Deck and I started making plans to meet up with each other.

He was not entirely keen on the wrevel itself—these parties, by reputation, were often raucous (something that would not necessarily daunt a shy person in cyberspace, where you had the time to sit back and think of a suitable rejoinder, but was a genuine consideration in this kind of a real life situation) and there was the threat of having photographs of oneself plastered all over the Web in the wrevel aftermath. He demurred that, in his own words, "like many fat men I dislike having my picture taken." But by this stage Deck was one of the best friends I had made on the Internet, and I would be, if not in the same country, at least on the same continent—something that, despite a seeming wealth of evidence to the contrary, was not an occurrence that was so common as to be dismissed as an opportunity to meet. So we compromised, and hammered out a Plan B. I would arrive in Vancouver the Friday before the wrevel, and so would he. We would meet up then, spend a few days together exploring the city, and then he would go home before the rest of the wrevel proper guests started arriving the following Friday.

The emails that flowed between us started taking on a feeling of excitement and euphoria. Towards the end of March, anticipating what was to come, I was writing things like, "Y'know, what is going to scramble me completely is hearing you talk <g> I think we all read emails in our own accents, so to speak. But that 'yeah' you just said, uttered in American <g> is probably different to anything I am expecting (and don't ask what I am expecting—how could I possibly know?"

By the first week of April we were crowing at one another that we'd got our tickets. On April 4 Deck wrote, "I WILL be in Vancouver on Friday. And you better be at the Barclay [Hotel] when I arrive! <g>" Days before I was due to depart, Auckland became threatened by a tropical storm of hurricane intensity; it was almost touch and go whether planes would be allowed to leave at all—"let it TRY and get in my way!" I muttered, following that particular flourish of bravado with the rash promise that I'd *walk* across the ocean rather than be cheated of my wrevel. And finally, a cryptic little one–liner on the eve of departure: "I'll see you in Vancouver."

Our schedule was practically military in its precision. I was due into Vancouver on the Friday morning, landing at some ungodly hour like 6 am (which Deck, the lark, always described as the best time of day) and I would then make my way to the bed and breakfast place I was staying in, somewhere in the suburb with the melodious name of Kitsilano. At three that afternoon I would be at the Barclay Hotel in Robson Street to meet Deck.

It was a strange case of déjà vu, in a way, because it had been me who had stayed at the Barclay on my previous visit to Vancouver; this time around I had chosen to upgrade to a more congenial B&B setting out in the suburbs but I had told Deck about the Barclay and he had managed to obtain a pretty good rate for the week he would be staying in Vancouver. For him, accommodation meant a place to sleep; any four walls around a convenient bed were fine. I needed an "atmosphere", somewhere pretty, and had once changed a hotel in mid–London after I had booked it months in advance when I got there and discovered that staying in the room they presented me with, even for as short a time as a few days, would give me terminal clinical depression. The Barclay was a central Vancouver hotel, neatly situated within walking distance of almost everything, and the rates were reasonable—it was, in fact, exactly the kind of hotel I would generally pick in a place like London. But there was something about the Barclay that somehow never quite gelled with me. It felt vaguely institutional, with its wide corridors, scuffed carpets that had seen better days, and plain room doors painted in oil paints and gleaming with a faintly ominous air in the vaguely dingy half-light in the back of a maze of corridors. I had described all this to Deck; he's dismissed them with a sigh of "Things!" which would become our running gag over the years. In my new chosen place of abode, I resided in a room with a skylight, on the top floor of an idiosyncratic wooden house in a leafy Kitsilano street. Deck would reel at the price I was paying for my "atmosphere".

I dawdled up and down Robson Street for almost two hours

before it was time for me to go and meet Deck at the Barclay. I had lunch at a café down the road, and it sat heavily in a stomach unsettled by a serious case of the butterflies; I had tanked myself up with coffee at one or another of the several Starbucks coffee shops on various Robson Street corners until I was humming like a too–tight violin string. I went into two bookshops and perused the book stacks for long mindless minutes without actually see-ing what I was looking at, running various possible scenarios of the coming meeting in my mind. Never before had I been this nervous about meeting a cyberfriend. I kept on running a "what if…" commentary in the back of my mind. "What if he hates me on sight? What if I talk too much? What if we have nothing to talk about? What if I had imagined all those wonderful emails we had shared? What if he was exactly the same as his email persona? What if he was *not*?"

I bought a book of Spider Robinson short stories and finally retreated into a comfortable lounge of another hotel a block of two up the street from the Barclay to wait. Someone approached and asked whether I wanted coffee; I was sorely tempted but I thought if I had another cup of coffee right then I would ei-ther throw up or *fly* to the Barclay without my feet touching the ground. So I sat there for some 45 minutes reading my Spider Robinson book; it had some 200 pages in it, and I actually fin-ished it before I tucked it into my capacious handbag and, in the grip of equal parts of terror and anticipation, made my way towards the Barclay.

Deck had not yet arrived, so I sat down in a strategic position where I could see the door and kicked my heels for another while of waiting. And then I saw…

When we were describing ourselves to one another initially, for recognition purposes, he'd said, "Think of Santa Claus."

I had thought he was merely trying to be amusing—he had all the requisite attributes, sure, but an expanded girth and a white beard do not a Santa Claus make. However, there was a quality about the man climbing the Barclay steps that was pure Christmas. We smiled at one another, in tentative but instant recognition, and then he dropped the bag he was carrying and hugged me. I hugged back, and as far as I can now recall that's when I started talking and didn't stop.

We went out for something to eat after he dumped his luggage in his room (I should have been warned. I had a serious pile of luggage clogging up my B&B closet; Deck arrived with a single small bag that seemed to contain all the necessities for a week's stay without even bulging). There was a place around the corner from the Barclay which served what I called pancakes and Deck insisted were crêpes, and that was where we found ourselves, me still talking like I had been wound up. In one of the rare pauses he smiled at me across the table and said quietly—I was to learn he said everything quietly—"This is okay. This works."

Something inside me relaxed, finally. It was, after all, going to be wonderful.

He walked me to my bus stop at some point and I caught a bus back to Kitsilano. We would meet up for breakfast the next day and start exploring Vancouver together. We went to visit such tourist traps as the Capilano Suspension Bridge and Stanley Park, where we got mobbed by peanut–seeking black squirrels in whom I took a great delight. We would stop for coffee at a convenient Starbucks every so often, and Deck later encapsulated this time as the moment he realised that trying to keep up with me, cup for cup, in my caffeine consumption would quickly give him a coronary, so he left me to drink my three cups of latte while he let his first cup grow cool (he liked his coffee cold) and sipped it slowly. We went out to a couple of wonderful dinners in a handful of Vancouver eateries. We met up with Stephanie Kwok, my co–conspirator, and we all went to pick up Jen, the wrevel hostess, for lunch; her double–take when she saw me ("What are YOU doing here???" she squealed when I turned up on her doorstep with a smugly grinning Stephanie) and her unfeigned delight when she realised that Deck, a stalwart in the group, might also be persuaded to attend her wrevel as another unexpected mystery guest were moments to treasure. The four of us went out to lunch and I listened to the conversation for a while until I finally said to the two Canadians, one of whom was from Calgary and the other from the west coast,

"You know, I am starting to finally be able to differentiate between the two of you by your accents."

As one, the three North Americans at the table turned to look at me loftily. It was Jen who said it, I think: "My dear, the only one at this table with an accent is *you*."

But over and above these encounters, Deck and I spent a lot of hours solely in each other's company. I discovered that what I had was a companion who was both a gentleman and a gentle man.

I also discovered that my *what if* litany of the pre–meeting anticipation hadn't quite gone far enough. What if we found that our friendship was… could be… more than that?

It was obvious, in the way he looked at me and the way he touched me, that what Deck felt for me was far more than simple friendship—and that he was ready to accept only the friendship, if that was all that I could offer. He had unequivocally handed me his heart, folded my hands around it gently, and told me that it was mine whatever else happened between us. As for me… it was now two years since John and I broke up, and I was still a fragile and emotional wreck. In the interim period of those two years, I had deliberately sought either solitude or the fleeting encounter which, from the outset, offered no longevity and no promises. The words "always" and "forever" had been tainted for me, I thought for good. I was an ex romantic; I believed in nothing. Nobody, but nobody, would come close enough to touch me that deeply again. And yet, when someone who truly cared for me asked if he could kiss me, for the first time in two years there was a shiver somewhere inside. It would take me to the edge of that festering pain I still carried within me, and beyond. There would come a time when I sobbed for a long time in Deck's arms, and then spent the better part of an hour trying to convince him that he had done nothing wrong, that the reason I was crying was not because he had done or said anything to cause it. But I also told him another thing. I asked him never to tell me he loved me. I did not want to hurt him by the fact that I could not seem to believe in that concept any more.

The week passed with astonishing rapidity. Ari, who was a friend to both of us but someone very special to myself, was due in on Thursday morning, and we were at the Barclay to meet him when he came there to rendezvous with us having arrived in Van-couver the previous night. Words were superfluous in this meet-ing and for the longest time Ari and I could just hug each other and grin. We went out to breakfast, and I remember walking down the street with an arm hooked to two of my favourite men in misc.writing, and feeling quite ridiculously happy. Sometime during the hours that the three of us spent together somehow the idea of Deck's staying on for the Wrevel metamorphosed from an arbitrary suggestion to firm intention. After a while Deck ex-cused himself, to make the necessary phone calls to ensure the continued survival of his cat back home and one or two other commitments that needed to be postponed, while Ari and I took off and spent a glorious spring day in Stanley Park, going off to the aquarium to see the killer whale, chattering in a manner that would make people at the wrevel, a few days later, demand to know whether we had *really* only just met or if we had in fact known each other from kindergarten.

The wrevel itself was a heady experience for me. Another good friend, Carol, from Toronto had also arrived early in order to spend some extra time with me; Deck had waited with me as I waited for her arrival in my B&B, where she would spend the night in a classic girls' slumber party before we both moved into the designated wrevel hotel for the duration of the party week-end. By this time I had acquired a case of the sniffles, and Deck, who swore by vitamins and mineral supplements, had already decreed a course of echinacea to ward off a cold. When Carol finally arrived (with one of the best introductory lines I've ever heard anywhere: "If you're Alma, I must be Carol!") Deck left us to catch the bus back to his own abode with an admonition to Carol not to keep me up too late as I was fighting a cold. Already he had a sense of responsibility for my wellbeing. Needless to say we disobeyed him shamelessly and stayed up until some ungodly hour just talking. Carol and I met up with Ari and Deck—a foursome that would quickly become an established "clique"— for coffee and breakfast on the Friday morning of the wrevel, and then we piled into a cab to go to the airport where the final members of the party were due to fly in that morning.

"So where are you all from?" asked the cabbie cheerfully, trying to make conversation.

The four of us just looked at one another and burst out laughing. It took some time to explain to the cabby that one of us was an American from Florida, one was a Finnish–born Swede, one was a Canadian of Welsh extraction from Toronto, and the last was a Yugoslav–born African–raised New Zealander—and that we had all come to Vancouver simply to have a party with people we had never met in real life before and whom we only knew as electrons from a shared newsgroup on the Internet. It was a while before the cabbie spoke again.

Aside from the four of us and the two Vancouver locals, Jen and Stephanie, the wrevel participants would include another Canadian from the city of Victoria and yet another, of Russian extraction, from Toronto; a long–haired New Englander whom I knew only by his Net moniker and found it unexpectedly difficult to address by his given name when asked to do so; a couple of Californians (one of whom was quite a well–known name in the speculative fiction world and was starting to make a reputation in Hollywood circles); and a member of the Sheriff's Department from Seattle. It's a good thing we had transportation arranged back to the wrevel hotel from the airport; our cabby would have fainted.

The astonishing thing was how well we all knew one another from the Net; some had already met before, at previous get–togethers, and others had only just made a RL acquaintance with one another, and yet the group of what on the face of it might have been a collection of complete strangers mostly behaved like they had found themselves at a family reunion. Someone's precious laptop computer and someone else's Internet connection (at long–distance dialup rates) were made available for posting party updates back to the envious non–attendees waiting to read about it on–group. That Friday night the party went on loud and long; the last people to drift off to bed were Carol, Ari and myself who finally did so at about four a.m. Around seven I was woken by a persistent ringing noise.

"Fire alarm test," I thought, somewhat irascibly (I had only had about three hours' sleep), and turned over to go back to sleep. But the noise persisted in its clamour, and I became aware of something else—a banging on the doors, a great commotion outside. Finally I gave up and emerged from the room to discover that the fire alarm was no drill. The facts of the situation, however, were soon to pass into misc.writing's history. The hotel we were staying at was chosen for the wrevel because every floor consisted of rooms clustered around a central atrium set up with comfortable wicker armchairs; there had been sufficient of us to rent an entire floor of the hotel, and the central area was perfect as a common party zone from which people, if they so chose, could withdraw into their own rooms. Breakfast was set up in this central sitting area also; and one of our number had decided to try toasting a bagel for her breakfast that morning. The bagel got stuck in the toaster and started emitting copious quantities of smoke, which triggered the alarm. The chaos potential of the whole thing was huge. Bleary–eyed people found themselves locked out of their rooms as they came out to investigate and heard the door snick shut with a smug finality behind them; others, who had gone to bed only scant hours before, emerged with too–serious expressions and dark glasses which spoke of somewhat tender dispositions. That night the bagel–burning culprit was sent off to bed by at least three people with the admonition,

"If you should feel the urge to toast yourself a bagel tomorrow morning… resist."

The wonderful wrevel came to a tearful end in due time, but our clique of the four musketeers was to share another day together—meandering happily into second–hand bookshops, making outrageous puns at each other and generally having a ball—before Ari, the first to leave, caught a cab back to the airport. Carol's taxi was not too far behind that. Waiting for her departure the three remaining musketeers, Carol, Deck and I, found a game of Scrabble in the sitting room of the B&B (to which I had returned post-wrevel) and had a game at which I, still the only person with an accent, managed to trounce the other two. Then Carol, too, was gone. Deck looked at me with the clairvoyant look I would come to know so well and said, "You'll see them again."

We took a walk across the bridge from Kitsilano towards downtown Vancouver. Across the water, in the dusk deepening into night, condo towers agleam with flickering lights marched in serried ranks away into the distance. I remember thinking, behind every one of those windows, controlling every one of those lights, is another human being, another life. I will never know them. And yet, the odds of my meeting one of them could not have been any greater than the odds of my meeting the man who walked beside me, holding my hand, who finally steered me into a "Death by Chocolate" restaurant to drown the post–wrevel withdrawal symptoms in rich dark chocolate sauce. Years later, talking about this walk, I was to learn that he had been thinking much the same thing as we walked across the bridge and gazed at the condo lights. Strange are the ways of the Internet.

We would conclude our visit to Vancouver by an outrageously expensive meal in the 'Prow' restaurant, under the 'sails' of Canada Place—we had a table next to a window, overlooking the harbour and the mountains above North Vancouver. Over a glass of wine, I tore out a page from the notebook I always carry in my purse and scribbled a poem:

> *Vancouver April*
> *Lights come on across the bay.*
> *The day sleeps at last.*
> *They light the candles*
> *At the tables—they reflect*
> *in a friend's eyes.*
> *What was future is almost past.*
> *It's painfully hard to believe*
> *in goodbyes.*

On my way to Deck's hotel on his last morning, I made an impulse stop at a florist's shop on my way and purchased a single rose. It was the sort of inchoate gesture that I, articulate as I am on many less important subjects, did not usually resort to—but it was a way of saying thank you. I chose a yellow rose, simply because those are my favourites, and did not know that Deck believed yellow roses meant friendship and that in giving him this one I was giving him quite a different message—*friends is all we will ever be.* We shared a last glass of wine in the hotel foyer as we waited for the taxi that would take him to the airport, and then I was waving him goodbye from the pavement before the hotel, and the car was disappearing down the street.

There was nobody to tell me, "You'll see him again."

CHAPTER 18:
"DO YOU TAKE THIS MAN TO BE YOUR WIFE…?"
ALMA

"WHENEVER YOU GET HERE, IT will be Christmas," Deck had said to me gallantly in one of our emails. Back in the southern hemisphere, where December 25 fell in mid–summer and New Year's Eve was often spent on the beach (something I, northern–born, never managed to quite get used to despite almost thirty years spent below the Equator), it was not uncommon for people to celebrate "mid–year Christmas"—it is too hot to either slave over or actually consume a full traditional Christmas dinner around actual Christmas–time down under. Many people compromised by having the turkey and all the trimmings at mid–summer, in June, when it was actually cold enough to believe in winter. Deck didn't do the turkey, but what *did* greet me as I walked into his house was a beautifully decorated Christmas tree in the window, complete with fairy lights and a pile of small parcels underneath.

"I've been saving them up," he said.

So he watched, grinning, as I sat on my heels on the floor in the middle of the living room like a kid on Christmas morning and tore the wrappings off the presents. Over and over again he showed that he listened to things I had said or implied. One of the books that was given as a gift was a non–fiction volume about wolves, my enthusiasm for whom I had expressed on many occasions. Another was a volume about the Everglades. Yet another was a fantasy writer's reference book, a genre he knew I had written at least one novel in. There were also books on the social history of America, as well as a gorgeously framed Navajo sand painting.

I was practically in tears by the end of it, moved by the planning and the care that had gone into this welcome. Deck's re-

sponse was almost perplexed, as though he could not comprehend why I couldn't understand why he did such things.

"I love you," he would say, repeating a simple phrase that covered all the thoughtful little things that he did, and he would
look at me almost reproachfully when I reacted by being moved
or touched by them. I did not yet know whether love would be
enough—what I did know was that my heart was brimming with
something warm and fine and that it was all this man's doing.
Finding out whether I could translate the theory of this into the
practice of living with him on a day–to–day basis was something
I still needed to find out—was, indeed, why I had come here in
the first place.

My birthday, July 5, was coming up fast; America celebrated its
own birthday the day before, of course, and generously provided
me with a magnificent fireworks display on the eve of mine. Deck
said he hadn't been to Fourth of July fireworks for years, so it was,
in a way, a new thing for both of us. I stopped off at an ice–cream
shop in downtown Stuart, where I spent almost five full minutes
making up my mind which one of their twenty-six ice cream
flavours I wanted, and got myself a splendid old–fashioned ice–
cream cone which melted over my hand and then walked down
the street towards the pier, where the fireworks were to be staged,
licking the sweet stuff off my fingers like a child. Perhaps the
illusion was easily created; I was wearing a pair of denim shorts,
a bright red t–shirt, and my hair in two plaited pigtails, a hair-
style I had abandoned as a regular "look" the first time I cut my
long hair, way back when I was twelve years old. I didn't feel
much older than that on this night; somehow the idea of being
simply being loved was growing on me, and the reflected glow
was making me feel young and invincible. I would write about
the experience on misc.writing, with somewhat unfortunate if
amusing consequences: the description of myself (shorts, pigtails,
joyfully waltzing onto the pier with my ice cream) was posted
through Deck's account, since I did not have a separate one of

my own. This meant that it was *his* name that headed this post in the group. We had several immediate responses begging us not to put mental images of Deck waltzing down a pier in shorts and pigtails into people's heads.

The fairy–lighted Christmas tree still stood in the living room window, probably to the confused consternation of the neighbours, by the time my birthday rolled around; we had thought to take it down then but we both liked the tree—and its implications—so much that we decided to leave it up a little longer. Coming home to "take down the Christmas tree" would rate as one of the more original excuses to leave yet another misc.writing wrevel that would be crossing our path in only a couple of weeks' time.

While planning this particular trip to the States, I did something that was quickly becoming a habit while travelling—I sent off the usual round of emails to people who were within easy (and inexpensive) reach of wherever I would be, in order to inquire about the possibilities of meeting up and setting faces to the names and the "electrons" with whom I had interacted on the Net. This time around one of the emails went to Rick O'Keefe, someone who had brought himself to my attention by being a quiet and unobtrusive but nonetheless stalwart support during the tough times of the past year. Despite not being, at this time, one of the "cyberbuddies" with whom I had a regular correspondence, he had forwarded snippets of information he thought would ease my anxieties or be of interest; he even sent a cyber–card for my birthday. I appreciated such people, more than they could possibly know. From previous on–group hints and clues I had gathered he lived in Florida; granted, it was on the west coast, but the distance did not seem insurmountable. So I fired off an email asking if he would be interested in a meeting, and the next thing I knew I found myself on a mailing list of people that included at least four other misc.writing people in the Tampa/Sarasota area, and a casual meeting was turning into a full–blown wrevel.

Initial dates mooted for the party hovered around the beginning of July, but since I would have only just arrived in Florida at that time and there were a number of other commitments by several of the potential attendees which could interfere with the proper attention that such a party deserved, the final date (agreed on only after my actual arrival at Deck's place) was set for the weekend of July 22, 2000.

In the meantime, Deck and I were settling into an easy shared routine. Our days seemed to fly past; hardly any would go by without one of us glancing at a convenient clock at some point and doing a double take when it became obvious that it was somehow, yet again, mid-afternoon and we had spent the morning doing some pleasurable (and sometimes even practical) thing together without noticing that the time was racing past. We were both increasingly aware of a strange feeling—the feeling that I had always been here, that nothing had ever been different.

I had come here to find out if it was possible for me to think about a long–term future with this man, and my questions seemed to be answering themselves. It was not only possible, it was being done, and I was enjoying it. As a child, I had found that I could spend sustained periods of time with a very limited number of people—a loner by nature, when forced into circumstances that necessitated prolonged spells of close companionship with people who did not meet my exacting if nebulous requirements I would, according to my mother, develop idiopathic malaises ranging from simple headaches to exotic complaints like earache or nausea for no particular cause. Here, in Deck's company, I was not only feeling happily content but "healthier" and more alive than I had done for a long time. He appeared to share the feeling; I would catch him grinning at me sometimes, with an expression of such unalloyed delight that I would find my lips quirking in an echoed smile before I became consciously aware that I was doing it. After all that we had weathered, together and apart, we…

fit. It seemed natural to spend time together. We did not crowd one another, but our personal spaces interlocked to form a shared quadrant where we were both comfortable and relaxed.

Attuned to all my foibles and small obsessions, Deck presented me with a small pink bear clad in a white t–shirt adorned with a heart pierced with a lightning bolt; I immediately dubbed the new plush Cupid, and it didn't seem too far–fetched to think that the *real* Cupid was putting the rest of his arrows back into his quiver and dusting his hands off with a satisfied smile. It certainly seemed like his job down here was done.

Four years and two months after we had first "met" and crossed swords in cyberspace, barely a week before what was now known as the Tampa Wrevel, Deck said to me over breakfast one morning, "Let's just get married."

I said, "We *could* announce it at the Tampa Wrevel."

෫෮

IT WOULD BE THE BOMBSHELL of the season on the newsgroup. The relationship had started there, after all. Although it had been under wraps for a very long time, it had actually been something of an open secret—at least since the publication of the Vancouver Wrevel pictures on the Web and the dead giveaway written in the expression on Deck's face every time he happened to be caught by the camera while looking at me. There were a handful of people who *knew*, although I was aware that there must have been any number of others who suspected. It somehow seemed fitting that a relationship born on this newsgroup be revealed there.

Deck's slow grin of complicity told me I was right.

We went to the courthouse on July 10 to find out about how to go about getting a marriage licence. The clerk at the counter handed us a booklet.

"You can't have one before you've read this, and attested to me that you are cognisant of what it says," she said.

So we took the booklet away to the nearest convenient space

and hunched over it.

"They don't seem to be very sanguine about marriage in this state," I muttered, after scanning the first page or so. The booklet appeared to contain mainly information on what to do should a couple decide to divorce. But it all seemed straightforward enough, and we took it back to the counter and took individual oaths that we had duly read it.

The official bent over her terminal, wrestling with the spelling of my name.

"Your first marriage?" she asked me.

I nodded, my voice suddenly gone.

"And your second," she said, typing up Deck.

"You've done this before," I said, glancing at him, partly in order to explain why I was clinging to his hand with both of mine.

"Not for a long time," he responded, with one of his slow smiles.

"That will be $75," the official said. "Cash, please, we don't take checks."

We actually had to empty both his wallet and my purse to scrabble together the requisite amount in cash, and half an hour after we left, licence in hand, Deck was still shaking his head and muttering about how the *last* time he did this it had been just a couple of dollars… and it didn't end there. It was a further $20 for the actual wedding ceremony itself.

ॐ

"THE CEREMONIES ARE PERFORMED HERE, at 10 am and 3 pm," the counter official told us. "Be warned, Friday is 'casual day' so if the possibility of being married by somebody wearing jeans offends you it might be better to choose a different day."

It didn't offend us, but since there was a mandatory waiting period of three days before we could marry the first day that we could pick for the ceremony was Friday the 13th. The date… was… well… But we took it.

The official aside, I now looked at my husband–to–be and put my foot down, gently but firmly.

"I will not insist on a tie," I said, "but you are *not* getting married in a plaid shirt."

Plaid shirts were something of a trademark; he was known by them. In the back of his wardrobe, however, we discovered a plain blue shirt that would match a pair of dress pants. So that was the groom sorted out. The bride was another story, and sifted through the clothes that she'd brought in search of something that would do duty as a wedding dress. The choice fell on a grey–blue semi–formal dress of almost Grecian simplicity, usually packed because it could be dressed up or down to suit most occasions, although I couldn't have known just how auspicious an occasion it would be called upon to grace this time. It was also useful, amongst other things, because it would take care of the "something blue" part of the wedding cantrip. "Something old" would be the joined wedding rings of my grandparents which I always wore on the middle finger of my right hand. "Something new" would be my own rings, and we set out to look for those on the way back from the marriage licence bureau.

In light of the short "engagement", we briefly considered waiving the engagement ring as such—however, especially after the beady question from Bonnie's daughter in Atlanta, I wanted a "rock", however small such a rock had to be in order to fall under the limited budget. I already wore up to six rings on both hands, and those were a fixture I never took off. I was usually festooned with other jewellery like bracelets and earrings. Deck expected me to spend an age looking for the perfect ring (where looks and price range had to be considered) but in fact it was in the first shop we called into that we found them—a delicate little set of wedding ring and engagement ring set with a tiny winking diamond chip. They were a trifle large, but I would get them sized later; Deck put the engagement ring on my ring finger immediately, but I would not wear the wedding band until I was entitled to it.

"Will you wear one?" I asked, a little diffidently. Men did, as a rule, where I came from—but it didn't seem to be as prevalent in the Western world.

"I don't wear jewellery," Deck said. "But your ring? Of course."

We picked up a wedding ring for him in the same shop where we found mine, and left it with the jeweller to be sized for Deck's finger.

It was a Monday, and that night, as usual, the Monday Nighters, the writing group that met at Deck's place every week, were due to come in for a meeting. They had been so involved in the development of both the novel Deck and I had written and, by default, in the development of the real relationship which ripened through the writing of it, that they reacted like family when they turned up and were presented with the ring on my left hand. It was Nina, one of the Monday Nighters, who eventually provided me with the "Something Borrowed" from the wedding cantrip—in a delicate allusion back to our co-authored novel, I would be wearing a pair of butterfly hair pins on my wedding day, and they would be graciously lent by Nina's daughter. All the Monday Nighters insisted on knowing when and where the wedding was, so that they could attend. Deck and I had originally planned something much simpler—him and me and the court official to stamp our marriage licence—but already we had half a dozen wedding guests right there. All of a sudden there were other people who needed to be told, and who now wanted to come along. One of them, Valerie, emailed us that she had even booked a table in a nearby restaurant for afterwards. Not only were we suddenly having a Wedding, we were presented with a Reception.

Thursday night I suddenly developed nerves. There was no sleeping; I was as wide awake as I was ever likely to be, eyes huge and full of nameless fears. I was playing "what if" again, just like back in Vancouver, except that this time the consequences were far more important. "What if I fail…?" Traditionally, Deck and I would have spent this last night apart, not seeing one another until the wedding the next day. Instead, we spent most of it wakeful, me shivering my way through a Universe of sudden brooding possibilities, him holding me in a tight bearhug and telling me there was no reason that everything wouldn't be fantastic, that there was a great and grand shared adventure about to begin the following day. Eventually, at some ungodly hour of the morning, he got up and made me hot cocoa laced with one of the herbal preparations ("for relaxation," he said) that he had in the house. I finally slept, and, as far as I know, did not dream.

The ceremony was scheduled for 3 p.m. that afternoon. In the morning we slipped out briefly to get some flowers that I could weave into my hair. This was a very impromptu wedding, in a lot of ways; those white flowers would be the only real giveaway that I went into that courthouse as a bride–to–be. We also got a single yellow rose, in memory of Vancouver, which the florist did up with baby's breath and white ribbon to serve as a bridal bouquet once apprised of its intended function. Back at the house, I paced; I did not want to start getting ready too early, leaving me all dressed up and nowhere to go yet and with time on my hands to sit and fret—and I did not want to leave things to the last minute, rushing headlong to my own wedding. But, finally, it was time to leave for the registry office—and I was as ready as I was going to be.

A handful of the Monday Nighters arrived early; so did others, Deck's friends who had known so much about me, for so long, that they treated my presence in his life at this moment as inevitable. From a small two–person event, the wedding had metamorphosed into an occasion attended by so many unexpected guests that the authorities had to open up a courtroom for us all to fit in there. Possibly flustered by the presence of so many people she had not expected to see there, the woman officiating at the ceremony—the same one who had issued us our wedding licence at the counter three days earlier, as it happened—started out by asking me very seriously whether I took Deck to be "my lawfully wedded wife". I said, "I suppose so…" The gathering dissolved into laughter; she looked a little startled but smiled, heaved a deep sigh, and started again. One of the guests told me later, at the reception, that I had got a bargain—a husband AND a wife in one package. But what was it I had really received at this ceremony?

Like all little girls, I had thought much about my wedding day when I was young. I started out by dreaming about fairy-tale princess dresses and husbands who were part fairytale prince and part movie star—beautiful, decorative, distant, and as fake as cardboard cutouts. As I grew up and grew older, especially after I turned down my own first marriage proposal at 19, I began to think about marriage in a different way—as something that had to continue past the glittering wedding which little girls never actually dream beyond. Gradually it became a marriage and not a wedding that I wanted for myself. Unlikely as my partnership with Deck was, as far as he was from the idealised poster–grooms of my distant childhood and youth, this was exactly what I was getting. Ours was a partnership based on friendship; "love," as he had put it in our novel, "is friendship caught on fire." This was a man who was first and foremost my friend, and I was surprised to realise how much that mattered, and how little of something this important I could lay claim to in my previous relationships. Perhaps it had something to do with the fact that the relationship had developed under the constraints that it had. I had learned to know Deck in a manner that was chaste and almost intellectual, and I was spared the initial euphoria of the 'falling in love' and then the devastation of disappointment and grief of the snuffing out of a flame that was pure passion. Was this something peculiar to Internet relationships? There was passion to be had there, too, for the taking—in fact, many a RL or Real Life marriage had sailed into rocky waters through one of the partners discovering

the allure of the realisation that the safest sex one could have under any circumstances could be engaged in by two parties linked
by a computer terminal.

℘

IT WAS AS MAN AND wife that we went to Tampa and the wrevel,
and it was eminently satisfying to see the initial shock and then
the genuine delight of our friends at our news. I posted the news
of the wedding on–group at the wrevel itself, and the good wishes
poured in—even a wedding present came in from another never–
met friend from Alabama, who was, and still is, a political "enemy" to both of us in the group. The cyberdance had gone the full
wheel—from strangers to friends to lovers and spouses; and the
responses we got from our net–friends (even those whom we still
only knew as nothing but electrons) were sometimes humbling.
At the conclusion of some 90 posts wishing us well from people
from Sweden, the UK, Israel, New Zealand and across the length
and breadth of the United States, the Last Real Marlborough
Man (the same character who had welcomed me to misc.writing
so many years ago) said, "what does it feel like to be so loved?"
We had made our lives a part of a shared community experience,
and it had been rewarding, and humbling. In the afterglow of
this euphoria, we now turned to practical aspects of setting up a
life together; there was still so much laughter and sheer delight
woven into this that I was moved to ask what, on the face of it,
was a perfectly reasonable question: "Is marriage supposed to be
this much fun?"

The post I wrote was this:

On Sat, 22 Jul 2000 15:38:32 -0400, "Alma" anghara@earthlink.
net wrote:

I had a rollercoaster few years in the second half of the nine-
ties. I moved to a new place (yet again), met a couple of guys
who, each in his turn, gave me a further blast back towards bed-

rock, and then sat back to lick my wounds; met misc.writing, and started being part of the community again. The road back to self-confidence has been a long and rocky one, but there are a few people without whom I would still have been at the beginning of it. Some of those, a majority, perhaps (this is bizarre - I depended in a huge way on the love and support of people I had never met...) are to be found on the Net. I have made some lifelong friends there. I am grateful.

One in particular has been an order of magnitude more important than the rest. I asked him not to speak of love to me and he went and showed me instead, in a thousand small loving ways, how much he cared in more than three years of emails and ICQ chats. He gave my life back to me, reached out across the miles and healed me of past hurts, gave me back the idea of the meaning of "always". And then, during a bitter conflict you all know very well, I stood in dire danger of breaking my heart and losing my soul over things I could do absolutely nothing about he bought both back for me in the coin of unconditional love and a level of support without bare survival would have been difficult.

Somewhere along the line, when he did finally tell me he loved me, I found myself able to say it back. All right, there were lots of problems. The age difference between us was huge (but, in the end, irrelevant); our politics often seemed poles apart (which would only make for an interesting lifetime); I was an only-child princess of doting parents, raised with a certain love of trappings, and he finds them irrelevant (except when they happen to be books)... we lived on different continents. But even that was solvable, and, in the end, solved.

I think that those of you who did not KNOW about this relationship could certainly make educated guesses, for quite some time now. There will probably be few who are really surprised to hear me say these things. But the man I speak of is Deck, and what I have to say here is, Reader, I Married Him.

I really don't think I need say any more. <smile>

❦

Those few chapters of the shared narrative, though—that was as far as "Cyberdance" ever got. That, and a detailed "Table of contents" of chapters to be written, who they would be written by, and what they would contain—here's what that looked like:

CHAPTER OUTLINES

CHAPTER ONE: OPENING THE CYBERDOOR
ALMA

IT SEEMS BEWILDERING NOW THAT there was a time that I knew nothing about the Internet at all, and that that time was less than five years ago. I had just moved to New Zealand from South Africa and was acclimatising to a new RL (or Real Life, as the Net people put it) place anyway—discovering the Internet and the cyberworld seemed an extension of an exploration of a new life. I was introduced to the Net—to email, the Web, and Usenet newsgroups—first by the Significant Other in my life at the time and then by other friends. I discovered the charm of making friends with people I had never met, first in the kind of public forum that a newsgroup is, and then, later, broadening and deepening relationships in personal email. I quickly learned that there were kindred spirits out there with whom I could establish lasting relationships. One of these, only just starting to bloom at this Age of Cyberinnocence that I was still going through, was with a man who would become my best friend, and then far more than that.

CHAPTER TWO: FOREVER AUTUMN
DECK

ALTHOUGH MY PRESENCE ON THE Internet as such did not pre-date Alma's to any significant degree, I had been toying with the precursor of the Net (the Bulletin Boards, or BBSs) for some time before I discovered Usenet and the Internet newsgroup culture. Alma and I first became aware of one another in misc.writing, the newsgroup we both called home, over a socio–political issue over which we held opposing views; once we called a truce and 'agreed to disagree' on this, we discovered that there was a whole universe of other things we could talk to each other about despite vastly different backgrounds and upbringing. I don't remember whether I first noticed her in the newsgroup as anything other than someone with a penchant for joyous wordplay and unbri-dled punaholism, but once we started corresponding in email, one on one, I was taken by her articulate intelligence and started taking a deeper interest in a woman whom I could see as becom-ing something important in my life. When I actually started to fall in love with her I cannot now recall, but I was probably more than halfway there by the time I received an email from her de-scribing a scene of English autumn that made me wish I could share the seasons of this woman's life.

CHAPTER THREE: WHAT IF...?
ALMA

ADRIFT FROM A RELATIONSHIP THAT was an important one in my life, I sought ways to escape from the memories. Christmas 1996 was spent in the Canadian Rockies, ostensibly on a skiing trip, but it was on this particular occasion that I had my first taste of meeting cyberfriends in real life, and I was hooked. Within misc. writing these parties, which became known as "wrevels", became something of a regular occasion, and although I found myself included in many of them via phone calls and such I wanted very much to extend the initial experience. So when a wrevel came up around Easter 1998, in Vancouver, I decided to go. It was to become a truly international wrevel, with guests from as far afield as New Zealand and Sweden—but an important part of the occasion, for me, was that Deck (who had become one of my best friends in the group by this time) and I made plans to meet in Vancouver. He did not initially wish to stay for the wrevel itself, but by the time the wrevel weekend arrived to conclude the week we had had together he had decided to extend his stay to give us a little more time to share. I'd met cyberfriends before, and so had he; but, for myself at least, never had I been more nervous about meeting one. It all turned out to be wasted worry, though. I'd run a gamut of "what if" questions just before we met; I was still doing that at the time we parted although the question had changed from "what if he doesn't like me?" to "what if there could be more...?"

CHAPTER FOUR: YELLOW ROSES
DECK

I HAD INVITED ALMA TO Florida but always thought it unlikely she would fly 8,000 miles to visit with a relative stranger in his home. When the opportunity came to meet her instead on neutral ground at a misc.writing party in Vancouver, to finally meet my cyberdance partner face to face, I impulsively, and rather uncharacteristically, decided to go. I found to my relief but not my surprise that in person Alma was exactly the same effervescent and intelligent woman I had been talking to for months—extended and intense conversation is remarkably revealing. We appeared to be connecting at a level and in a way I had hoped for but never thought possible. Our budding relationship was briefly interrupted by the misc.writing party where I was not surprised to discover that there was little difference between the cyberspace personas and the RL individuals. The conversation in misc.writing, as in most newsgroups, while not as intense as the email correspondence between Alma and me, was nearly as revealing of character and personality. When the party ended, Alma and I resumed our curious and cautious courtship, the RL counterpart to our cyberdance. But she brought me a gift the last morning I was to spend in Vancouver, a yellow rose. I thought it was a gentle and gracious way of saying: this far and no further. I had been taught, I 'knew', that roses do tell—red roses of love, yellow of friendship. I was disappointed but resigned. On the flight home I wrote a poem ending with the lines, "Whatever is to be/ We will always have Vancouver." I was not about to give up our deep cyberspace friendship. I enjoyed our daily emails and measured my days by them.

CHAPTER FIVE: THE YEAR IN BETWEEN
DECK

THE MONTHS SPED BY AFTER Vancouver while we pursued separate lives. But our emails became more frequent, first to several a week, then one a day, then often several a day. We discussed the trivial and the profound. We argued about books and music, TV shows and movies. Alma was appalled when I called one of her favorite books, *Gone With the Wind*, an overblown potboiler that tried to justify the unjustifiable, the institution of slavery. I told her I wrote mysteries and she noted that she found them boring. She told me she wrote fantasies and I warned her I hadn't read one in years. I told her I'm a feminist; she claimed they were all bra burners. We discussed what we would save from our homes in the midst of a fire. We discussed each other's post in misc.writing and talked about other newsgroups we were active in. I told her about my adult education classes and freelance work, and she discussed her work and problems in the workplace. In short, we were feeling each other out in the eons old dance. In the meantime I met another woman from misc.writing when she came down from Canada to a book fair in Miami. We had a delightful afternoon together, talking about all our mutual cyberspace friends, Alma most definitely included, although I didn't quite admit my growing interest in her. Our emails were becoming an addiction, something that Alma alluded to when I told her about helping a friend buy and setup a computer for his wife. Four hours after we had bought it, the wife was sitting before deep in conversation in a chat room. Alma wryly asked me if I had warned them how that chat could become downright compulsive and how little they would see each other from then on. At the same time, of course, we were doing the opposite—using the computer and the Internet to make the connection that allowed us to spend more and more time in each other's virtual company. A year slipped by almost imperceptibly. And then everything changed for both of us.

CHAPTER SIX: ROLLERCOASTER
ALMA

THE REST OF 1998 WOULD prove to be a rollercoaster year. I would deepen cyber–relationships in a number of new ways, including discovering "chat"—real–time communication almost as good as a phone call and infinitely more immediate than even email—and mediate in crises of the heart half a world away. I would get involved in a distracting wrangle following a minor car accident. I would lose my full–time editorial job through redundancy, and take up first freelancing and then part time employment at the Auckland University. At Christmas 1998 my friend Carol from Toronto, one of the Vancouver "musketeers", would come for a visit to New Zealand, and she, I and Maggie (the friend who introduced me to misc.writing in the first place nearly two years before) would travel down to the South Island to research a novel which Maggie and I had been collaborating on for a couple of years now in happy procrastination. It seemed that my links to the cyberworld were getting more and more solid, as Net friendships metamorphosed into rich personal relationships—and, amongst these, the one that was growing between Deck and myself was certainly shaping to be an important one to me to the extent that, with the daily emails, the ICQ chats and the occasional phone call, I found it increasingly hard to imagine a life that did not include him. He was still under the Vancouver ban on speaking of love to me—overtly, that is. If I cared to read between the lines, there was plenty there to tell me what his feelings were. And yet, the barriers that had always been between us were not growing any less substantial—the age difference, the distance, the disparity in political and world views, my own armour against any romantic possibilities. But as the new year came and went, darker clouds would loom on my horizon and quite effectively distract me from dwelling on any and all other preoccupations—something almost unbelievable in the closing years of the second millennium: the Western world would declare war on the country of my birth.

CHAPTER SEVEN: FAMILY AT WAR
ALMA

WHEN THE WAR STARTED, MY family, with limited contact with our relatives back in the old country, turned to the Internet for information. It was devastating, the helpless feeling of being too far away and too isolated to be anything more than just an observer on the sidelines, but if it had not been for the Net and its possibilities it would have gone much harder with us all. Ignorance and misinformation always make any burden heavier. But not only is the Internet a new communications medium connecting people, it is also a treasure trove of information—perhaps the last bastion where anything and everything is still accessible, without bias or censorship. This may still change, but for now the Internet is still too large and too free spirited to be controlled by any one entity. In March 1999, when the mainstream media provided only officially sanctioned information, the Internet was the only place where alternative viewpoints on the conflict in Yugoslavia were available. If the Gulf War was in some respects the first television war, this conflict was the first cyberwar and we watched as the dogfights unfolded in cyberspace. And then, slowly...

CHAPTER EIGHT: NET WARS
ALMA

...I STARTED TALKING ABOUT IT on misc.writing, my home group. It was a place that was dominated, like much of the Internet is through sheer weight of numbers, by Americans, and I might have expected to be targeted as the Enemy there when I stepped up to the line and started debunking "official" information. Instead, while I did get plenty of "enemies" (both high–calibre, principled people who simply believed in different dogmas and the poisonous cranks who made the whole thing personal and dangerous), I also got an unprecedented outpouring of support. While the bombs were falling on the country where I had been born, I was fighting a rearguard action in my home newsgroup where the discussions could, and did, get quite heated on occasion. It was obvious, to those who knew me on the Net, that I was taking the whole situation hard. Deck was a rock, sending me concerned emails, cards, and on one occasion a "Care package" of chocolate which never arrived, probably being confiscated by some hungry postal worker or customs official. He opposed the war for reasons of his own, and in the newsgroup battles he was a staunch ally. There were others in the group—Americans, mostly—without whom it would have been difficult to endure the strain of the war. The Net was precisely that for me at this time, a safety Net, a place where I could go and get surrounded by friends offering moral support. I had still only met only a fraction of the people I knew, and now, depended on—and yet people I sometimes barely knew sent me information, support and understanding.

CHAPTER NINE: A NOVEL SOLUTION
DECK

I WAS STUNNED AND ANGERED at the Clinton/NATO assault on Yugoslavia and initiated what became an increasingly virulent debate in misc.writing. At times it appeared that it was Alma and I against the world, with everyone else concluding the war was both good and justified. In an email discussion with a friend who knew my feelings for Alma, I expressed both my concerns about how the war was affecting her, and my own distress at what I thought was a hopeless one-sided romantic attachment. She sent a list of suggestions, including a novel idea: Why not write a short story involving correspondence between a Serbian woman and an American man? She meant it as a palliative to sooth my wounded ego, but I immediately saw greater possibilities. I fired off an email to Alma, suggesting that we write a novel using that approach. I admitted to some concern that "On a personal level, we might open some wounds, find some areas where we aren't in as total agreement as we have been up to now." But then I added: 'But I think it has too much potential for good to ignore without at least exploring the possibility." By 'potential for good' I meant put a human face on the war and perhaps open some eyes. I wasn't sure how we would end it, and said so. "The ending—I don't know. A love story? The two characters falling in love? If so, what then? Or some twist that makes love impossible (too big an age gap perhaps <g>)? Or to add a poignant twist, make it a tragedy with the pair falling in love and planning a life after the war with the woman being killed at the end by a NATO bomb, leaving the man to try to understand what it was all about?" After some hesitation, Alma agreed to give it a try. The novel, *Letters from the Fire*, is written as a series of email messages between our characters and we wrote it the same way. I would send an email from my character Dave, and Alma would respond to it as her character Sasha. Because of the time difference between Florida and New Zealand, we were in effect writing around the clock. I would write a 'Dave' message and go to bed. When I awoke in the morning, there would be a reply from 'Sasha.' A month after we started the novel we were halfway through it. Alma approached the editor of HarperCollins in New Zealand and he asked to see what we had done. We finished it on June 6, barely two months after we started it, three months after that it was in bookstores in New Zealand and Australia. It was a satisfying and novel solution, and one that led to a switch in our relationship.

CHAPTER TEN: OUT OF THE FLAMES OF WAR
ALMA

WHILE BOTH THE ACTUAL WAR and the flame wars in misc.writing were still in full swing, Deck's suggestion that it might be a worthwhile idea if he and I wrote a story about the situation initially brought nothing but an instinctive recoil from me—the whole thing was too close, too painful. But then I cautiously said we should maybe give it a try. For my part, my section of the book was not so much written as wrung from me. The passion and pain gave the narrative the sort of strength which made a New Zealand publisher I knew ask for "the rest of the manuscript" when I showed him the initial part of the emerging novel and asked if he would be interested in something like that. He was, and, as it turned out, with reason. Almost half the book's initial print run was sold within the first three months of publication. We had a success on our hands. More than this, the book served another purpose. It was a love story set against the backdrop of war. Love stories require action and reaction. Perhaps for the first time since we met and I forbade him to mention the word "love" to me, Deck had licence to tell me (even if he WAS in the persona of his character in the novel) how he really felt... and I would have to respond. I found it a lot easier than I thought I might. I suddenly realised that a door I had thought permanently locked and sealed was now standing invitingly ajar. A choice lay before me.

CHAPTER ELEVEN: "OH GOD. I THINK I JUST SAID YES."
DECK

"DAVE" HAD OPENED THE LONG–CLOSED door. While Alma had begged me not to speak of love, our characters in *Letters from the Fire* had fallen in love, and Dave could not be gagged. When the book was finished and moving through the publishing process, Alma and I returned to the Real Life of cyberspace and resumed chatting in ICQ every day. Alma admitted that things had changed, and she no longer feared my declaring my feelings for her. She cautiously reciprocated, but there was still a reserve there. On June 14, 1999 she told me we needed to talk seriously. My heart sank, particularly when the following conversation took place:

> *<Deck> I said, or implied, that I feared that you were/are attempting to convince yourself that you are in love with me out of some sense of obligation; I hate to think that possible, but I fear it is.*

*<Alma> <smile> Deck, I did nothing of the
sort because I never did tell you I was in love with
you. I said I loved you. that is different.*

*<Deck> ok, I decided in my own mind at
some recent point that you have moved from loving
me to being in love with me; I was just mistaken,
wishful thinking.*

<Alma> oh god.

*<Deck> don't cry; you can't force what you
don't feel; nor do you need to feel bad about it....*

At that point the ICQ connection was broken, as it not infrequently is. When we finally reconnected what seemed like hours later (it was a few minutes) Alma told me I was misinterpreting what she was trying to say, that she loved me but had simply bypassed the infatuation stage that most people think of as 'falling in love.' Once this was cleared up, I worked up my courage and asked her to marry me. She mused about the fact that an Internet friend was a minister, authorized to perform marriages, but was still talking around the point. Finally, I asked: "What are you trying to say?"

"Oh, God," she answered. "I think I just said yes."

CHAPTER TWELVE: GOING HOME
ALMA

EXHAUSTED, TROUBLED, WORRIED, RELIEVED—WE WERE all of those by the time the war "ended". The frailty of existence had been brought home to all of my family to an unprecedented degree. The last time the clan had seen each other had been back in 1991—that, in terms of what had happened in Yugoslavia in the intervening period, was ancient history. My mother and I made plans to travel home to see family, and to see what kind of damage had been wrought. She would stay a couple of months; I would stay for a while, and then I would do another of my Internet trips—I would return to New Zealand via Sweden (visiting Ari) and the United States (taking Deck up on that long–ago invitation to stay with him in Florida). The trip to Yugoslavia was emotionally draining, and it would take the rest of my journey, and then some, to recover from what I found there. But I had a haven of inestimable value on my return journey. Deck and I explored Florida, finally getting to the Keys which he had promised me... was it really *years* ago?... We survived a hurricane together, waiting for it to hit while he taught me how to play poker. We spent some pretty intense time together, this time in his own home territory. It was very humbling to realise how many people knew about me, and how *much* people knew about me. It was inevitably brought home to me just how much a part of his life I had become... and how much a part of mine HE had become in return. But then the week was over, and I was in Auckland again, 8000 miles away. And this time, it was *hard*.

CHAPTER THIRTEEN: EYE OF THE STORM
DECK

WHILE ALMA WAS SWIMMING WITH the dolphins in the Keys, I got a taste of what might happen if we were to become a serious pair. A woman watched as I shot pictures of Alma with a dolphin in her lap and asked, "Is that your daughter.... wife?" She had caught herself almost instantaneously, but the thought had been there. "Wife to be," I answered, expressing a wish but not what I thought was reality. However, Alma and I had become intimate and while I didn't think this could change anything in the long run, it clearly changed the way we reacted to each other. We were waiting for a table in a restaurant when a man entered, glanced at us in passing, and then did a perfect double-take. His head whipped back to us, and then, bemused, he quickly looked away. It was only then that I realized we had been sitting with my hand casually lying on her shorts-clad legs. At the Orlando airport as we waited for Alma's departure flight, she impulsively slipped one of her rings onto her left ring finger and said she wished she could marry me then and there. But there was something theatrical about the gesture and I didn't think that at heart she meant it. I watched her leave with foreboding, fearing that I would never see her again in RL, that we would return to a cyberbuddy relationship. And even that, I was sure, would someday end. For the next several months we continued much as before, except that the emails had given way to ICQ messages. ICQ is a form of instant email exchange, the equivalent of a phone conversation conducted by typing. It is more intimate, but like most phone or RL conversations it is more chatty, less thoughtful. Paradoxically, while I delighted in the intimacy, I missed the long and often introspective exchanges we'd had in email. At 4 or 5 a.m. each morning, Alma and I would chat in ICQ before she went to bed and I started my writing day. She was a central part of my life now, an inseparable part. I couldn't really imagine life without her.

CHAPTER FOURTEEN: NOTHING TO FEAR BUT FEAR ITSELF
ALMA

I HAD HAD MARRIAGE PROPOSALS at 19 and at 26; both of them I turned down, for reasons that seemed eminently sensible at the time. At 19 I had considered myself to be too young to even consider the idea; at 26 the circumstances were not right, and I balked. I stayed friends with the first would–be husband to this day, and probably would have done the same with the second had I stayed in South Africa. But then I had hit thirty, and then thirty five. My parents and I still lived together—a state of affairs not uncommon back in the culture where I came from but something odd and strange in the Western world. I had trained for one career but pursued another, one that was not making me rich; part of the living arrangements was simply the fact that I never quite seemed to be able to break away and continue to keep myself in the manner to which I had become accustomed. And I had become... complacent, in a way. Life was comfortable. I had never needed to become "domesticated"—while I could follow a recipe I rarely cooked in the kitchen where my mother reigned. I lived in cozy comfort with my books and my music and my writing; I had two beloved pets. I had everything I ever wanted. And yet, during a medical crisis where I had been taken to be treated – by my mother – I found myself wishing with a surprisingly savage fury that I could spend my time with someone who wanted to spend it with me as opposed to someone who was obliged to spend it with me. I knew, of course, that my parents doted on me like only the parents of an only daughter can dote—but I wanted more than that. I wanted a partnership. It was time, past time, to have my *own* family, and not be merely part of someone else's. But my doting parents could not be expected to understand the cyber–relationship that was shaping this urge. I wrestled with the dilemma of being all things to all people while my parents lived in the conviction that nothing would ever change in our lives and Deck, half a world away, waited patiently while I came to terms with the need for that change.

CHAPTER FIFTEEN: "I *WISH* YOU WERE IN THE SAME TIME ZONE..."
DECK

PATIENCE IS AN IMPRECISE TERM. I didn't want to pressure Alma to move faster than she comfortably could. I was well aware of what it would mean to her to uproot herself from her family, to leave her beloved pets behind (at least for a time), to move to another continent, and to face an uncertain financial future. I was living on Social Security, a minuscule pension from the Miami News, and an embarrassingly small freelance income. Unless we could build a book-writing career, an increasingly difficult feat in the age of megalith publishing mergers, Alma would have to get a job. And at some point, we'd have to figure out what was required for immigration. That latter point was moot until Alma made the decision to actually come to me. She had agreed to marry me, but that was an abstraction until she had made the emotional decision to move. Our lives were now entwined and we probably talked more together every day than 99 % of the couples on the planet, up to three hours a day. But it was nearly all done in email and ICQ. Not infrequently the latter was iffy. Many conversations were interrupted two or three times as the system froze, including the ICQ conversation in which Alma had agreed to marry me! "The course of true love never runs smooth—in ICQ Internet chat," I said one night with a sigh. Our relationship was totally based on a concept, a technology that had existed in its current form little more than a decade. The time differences could make for exhausting compromises. I normally got up about 6 a.m. But now I was getting up and 4 and 5 a.m. to make connection with Alma a half world away. At one time I sighed and said earnestly: "I wish you were in the same time zone."

CHAPTER SIXTEEN: ALL I WANT FOR CHRISTMAS
DECK

CHRISTMAS OF 1999 WAS APPROACHING and Alma still hadn't made a decision. I told her of my longing that she be here by the holidays, but she said that was impossible. I told her that I'd have a Christmas tree up whenever she arrived. While a holiday move wasn't going to happen, I did think it was time to try to nudge her into making a definite commitment and suggested a March deadline. She was non-committal and I tried not to push. We were making occasional phone calls in addition to our daily three-hour ICQ chats, and exchanged countless snail mail and cyberspace cards. The new year came, and things were as undefined as ever. Sometimes I despaired that nothing was going to happen and our grand cyberdance would come to an end, not with a bang but a whimper. But our chats sustained me, and we both still had separate lives to lead. We played around with other book projects, including one that I thought had a lot of promise—a non-fiction book about communications in cyberspace. While literally hundreds of books were being written about the Internet, most of them focused on the business possibilities of the World Wide Web. Very few looked at the way the Internet was revolutionizing the way people were finding each other in chat rooms and newsgroups, keeping in touch with friends and family through email, and finding romance, as we had. In addition, we sketched out plans for a humorous look at a fictional newsgroup. Several more months went by before Alma told me she had decided to make another trip to the U.S. While this wasn't the move I was hoping for, the one that would bring her to me permanently, she did say that she had arranged it so that we could have several weeks together. Virtually the first thing I did on hearing her plans was to put up the Christmas tree and decorate it. I'm sure my neighbors, and passing cars, were a bit confused at the lighted Christmas tree in my window, but no-one said a word. I wrapped a number of gifts I had been collecting for months and put them under the tree. And then I waited impatiently.

CHAPTER SEVENTEEN: "IT'S A GRAND CANYON..."
ALMA

"IT'S A CANYON," DECK SAID at one point about the potential of our relationship, "but it's a *grand* canyon." He painted a picture of the possibilities, of life that would not necessarily be a bed of roses but would certainly be a shared adventure; I carried on vacillating, reluctant to abandon the only life I had ever known, reluctant to commit to setting sail into uncharted waters even if they *were* full of promise. We were friends—Deck was probably one of my best friends ever by this stage—and this was a solid ground to build on. To build *anything* on, even marriage. But I was learning about Deck's ability to fish silver linings out of the darkest clouds, even as he learned about mine to wrap clouds around silver linings. We had spent maybe three weeks in each other's company, in real life, so far if one totted up our meetings up to this time. Those meetings had been wonderful, but they had been brief, and had been spent in the spirit of 'holiday'. Perhaps now was the time to find out if we could handle a longer period of time together. Still following my tradition of meeting up with Internet friends on every recent journey of my life, I set off for America once again to spend some time with Deck, to see if this thing could actually work. On the way, I dropped in for a visit to two of my misc.writing friends, one of whom took me off for an excursion... to the Grand Canyon. I stood at the edge of this natural wonder, breathless at the beauty and power of it, and found myself thinking that if Deck's words had been right there could be worse ways to live one's life than discovering this sort of awe and wonder every day...

CHAPTER EIGHTEEN: "DO YOU TAKE THIS MAN TO BE YOUR WIFE...?"
ALMA

YET ANOTHER INTERNET PARTY PLANNING fever had hit the States with my arrival there, and almost the entire misc.writing contingent from Florida decided that while I was in the area, a party was mandatory. The date for what became known as the Tampa Wrevel was set for one weekend in the second half of July, long before I left Auckland, and firmed to July 22 by the time I arrived at Deck's a few days before the end of June. When we had talked about this visit, it was originally thought that I would be there around the previous Christmas—but other things had intervened and it had kept getting put further and further back; however, he had promised at one point that he would keep up his Christmas tree for me, and when I arrived the tree was up, complete with a bunch of little parcels, Christmas presents (books and suchlike) that he had accumulated for me. We left the tree up until my birthday, July 5, to the probable consternation of the neighbours. Our days seemed to fly by; not a day would go past without one of us exclaiming that it could not possibly be 3 p.m. already. We were both increasingly aware of a strange feeling—the feeling that I had always been here, that nothing had ever been different. "Let's just get married," he said, and I finally said yes. So we got our licence, and told a friend, then another friend, and before long we found ourselves having to change our original plan for a quick registry office wedding with just ourselves and the officiating Justice of the Peace to an occasion attended by about fifteen people, including all of the "Monday nighters", the writing group which met at Deck's weekly and which had been so instrumental in *Letters from the Fire* that they had made the acknowledgments page.

Perhaps a little flustered by the sheer number of unexpected guests, the official who was in charge of the ceremony fluffed her lines and asked me if I took Deck to be "my lawful wedded wife."

I was told later at the party, a friend had arranged for us at a nearby restaurant (complete with a totally unexpected wedding cake) that I had got a bargain—a husband AND a wife in one package. It was as man and wife that we went to Tampa and the wrevel, and it was eminently satisfying to see the initial shock and then the genuine delight of our friends at our news. I posted the news of the wedding on–group at the wrevel itself, and the good wishes poured in—even a wedding present came in from another never–met friend from Alabama, who was, and still is, a political opponent to both of us in the group. The cyberdance had gone the full wheel—from strangers to friends to lovers and spouses; and the responses we got from our net–friends (even those whom we still only knew as nothing but electrons) were sometimes humbling. At the conclusion of some 90 posts wishing us well from people from Sweden, the UK, Israel, New Zealand and across the length and breadth of the United States, the Last Real Marlborough Man (the same character who had welcomed me to misc.writing so many years ago) said, "what does it feel like to be so loved?"

We had made our lives a part of a shared community experience, and it had been rewarding, and humbling. In the afterglow of this euphoria, we now turned to practical aspects of setting up a life together; there was still so much laughter and sheer delight woven into this that I was moved to ask what, on the face of it, was a perfectly reasonable question: "Is marriage supposed to be this much fun?"

CHAPTER NINETEEN: COMING TO AMERICA
ALMA/DECK

NOT BISCUITS, BUT COOKIES; NOT scones, but biscuits; not pan-cakes, but crepes. There was a whole new vocabulary to learn, and that was just in the kitchen. There was also the need to come to terms with gallons, miles, and Fahrenheit. There seemed to be no unit in this country that Alma could understand. On top of this there was the fact that people in the USA drove on the "wrong" side of the road, and that nobody seemed capable of giving an actual date—Americans functioned from holiday to holiday ("It'll be ready by Labor Day"). And these were just the beginning. We had to start from scratch—taking into account that Alma had never actually lived with a man for any length of time before this, and Deck had been living alone for what seemed to be an unspeakable number of years. We had to get used to living with one another. On the whole it proved remarkably easy to achieve. We celebrated American holidays (the Fourth of July, Halloween) and Deck took a childlike delight in Alma's discovery of her new country. We would go out to restaurants and hold hands, spend hours of companionable silence at local parks and recreation areas, take in the occasional movie; we found ourselves remarkably content. The advent of the new year, the new century and the new millennium would find us making plans for a shared lifetime, transposing the cyberdance courtship into a warm and treasured real life relationship to take with us into the future.

 ❦

THE FUTURE SEEMED SET AND solid. But we never got there.

2003 had other plans for us. 2003 was the year of change, of our big move—but before we reach that milestone, let me just linger in these early years for just a moment longer, and show you some pieces of the early puzzle.

First, the threads from that Vancouver encounter—and then a visit I paid to Florida, later.

The time he delivered me back to the B&B where I was staying with my friend, and told her, very seriously, very sincerely, "I think she may have a cold coming on. Echinacea is good for that. Take care of her." (that was the moment, I think, that I felt those wings fold around me, and I knew I was safe, I was treasured, I was protected…)

The way we would both stop and sigh when we looked down a cross street in Vancouver and caught sight of the mountains.

Our quick side trip to Whistler.

That wretched yellow rose that took so long to straighten out (it was a titanic misunderstanding in the Language of Flowers, where I gave him a flower I loved with no further subtext and he interpreted it as the Yellow Rose of Friendship and a hint that we could never be more than that…)

The way he listened to me, and took me seriously, and when I told him that I was on the wretched edge of that bad, bad break-up and that I needed a friend more than any kind of romantic interest and that he should not speak to me of love… he did not speak to me of love. He just showed me, every moment, every chance he got.

The little creperie in the side street where we first talked and talked and talked.

The way I always could trust him, I could talk to him about anything.

On the Florida visit, I remember that the flight was horribly delayed for some reason, and I ended up finally arriving some six hours after I should have done by the itinerary. He had come to the airport in Orlando to pick me up and had waited there for all those hours until I finally staggered off the plane—I stayed awake in the car long enough to help navigate out of the airport maze and then I simply fell asleep, and he drove for two hours from Orlando back to his home in silence with me in the car. When we got there he woke me, and I stayed awake just long enough to transfer from the car to a bed and keeled right over again. And in the morning, he was up and waiting when I finally woke up, with breakfast, and coffee, and a smile. And he took me out to show me his world, and show me TO his world.

And then there was the trip to the Everglades, to the Keys. He introduced me to gator tail and Key Lime Pie. He took me to swim with dolphins, and watched me do it, and shared every moment of that joy. He introduced me to hurricanes.

Then I went back home, to New Zealand, and the correspondence and the discovery continued. The daily chats on ICQ lengthened and deepened.

He kept transcripts of all of them—ALL OF THEM—all except the very important one, the one where he finally asked in a convoluted and diffident way if I ever would consider being with him, and I said, "well, as proposals go…"—the power went out at a crucial time, and he did not manage to save that one. I always teased him afterwards that he actually never did have a record of any such interchange, and he made it all up.

Our shared lives were yet to begin properly. But before they did… and just as they did… there were three special years.

❧

1999—bringing my soul back from the brink of perdition.

THE LAST YEAR OF THE previous millennium, the previous century, was stormy.

My native Balkans had been in the process of disintegrating—

sometimes bloodily—for some time. But in 1999 the United States—acting according to a sometime Secretary of State's appalling statement that it was ridiculous to have the kind of military that the US boasted without, you know, USING it—decided to do its usual thing, ignore inconvenient facts, and forget history, and find a place to aim that military—squarely at my native land, at Serbia. The US had its own reasons, and they were not clean—no war was declared because they had no basis to declare one but all of a sudden Serbia was being bombed by American planes, dropping ordnance on everything from transportation and utility grids to the occasional idiotic blunders like blowing up the Chinese embassy in Belgrade. I—together with my family—watched it all from far away, in New Zealand, and I wept as I watched the bridges of my childhood being blasted away for no reason except that those bombers COULD. People online whom I thought were my friends began to snarl at me because of who I was and where I was born—ignorant and irrationally 'patriotic', absolutely certain their country could do no wrong, they waded in screaming "USA! USA!" and everyone who got in the way of their blundering hobnailed boots be damned.

I fought back, with words, with facts, with passion, online—in that world I had made my own. But I was beating my bloody fists against what seemed like a brick wall, sometimes.

One man stood by me, absolutely. Deck.

A mutual online friend from Misc.writing who watched all of this, Carol, suggested we should "write a book together".

It was from these inauspicious pained beginnings that "Letters from the Fire" was born—perhaps the world's first email epistolary novel. It would give me a chance to tell the story—the real story—but in order to do this I needed a foil, someone to convince—and so we took on characters, Deck and I, and began writing emails to each other "in character". This was a book written around the clock because he was in Florida and I was in New Zealand and one of us was literally going to bed as the other rose from one, which meant that the emails were flying 24 hours a day. Of the two of us, he took the harder path—because part of his "character" involved BEING there to convince, which meant that he had to be a mouthpiece for many ideas which he did not himself espouse or share—I wrote my own character, Sasha, from the white heat of the heart of my own sense of loss and betrayal (and Deck told me, much later, that there were times that he wondered if this book was going to be the end of us, after all...). "Letters" was powerful, and passionate, and pure—we dedicated it "To the victims of war: Human Beings, Human Constructs, Human Ideals"; it was the most anti-war "war" novel that it is possible for a book to be; and it was also our own truth, the emergence of our own love story, which is in retrospect so clear and so obvious that on re-reading the book years later I was astonished at how unafraid we were to show the world our innermost selves. It created and cemented so many shared thoughts, ideas, images; his character spoke of sending "butterflies" as loving thoughts, and many years later I would pour some of Deck's ashes into a pendant shaped like a tiny blue butterfly, something I could put on a chain and wear as a necklace, so that he could still come with me anywhere I went. I found myself recognizing words, phrases, from that book—they shaped our lives in the aftermath, with the spirit of this book being a backbone of our relationship. It cemented us to one another. He loved me enough to do this for me—to give me the platform I needed, to assume the face of the "enemy" I needed to convince and to show that such an "enemy" could be convinced—he handed me love and hope with both hands, and I took it. I took it all. And I knew that I was willing to give everything I could back in return. I looked at him and I saw someone who would always be with me, no matter what—in the crucible of that war that we wrote about our own love was tempered, and what emerged... was good steel.

It was less than year after "Letters" saw the light that I finally took that final plunge.

ↂ

2000—when I finally crossed the pond for good, and there were the Florida years.

I CAN BARELY BEGIN TO describe to you how it felt to arrive into a strange place as a total stranger… and to discover that random people greet you with utter recognition, because they've already heard so much about you from the man beside you, beaming at a wattage that is almost impossible to look at without protective eye gear. "Oh, so *you're* his Alma…" became a refrain. At his favourite breakfast restaurant to which he took me. At his life story classes, where I sat in, and discovered that half the class already knew my own life story. With every friend and acquaintance of his that I met.

He told me that he would understand completely if I pulled out—right until the time I said "I do"—but after that it would all work out. He knew it would. I trusted him on that.

I loved being with him—but (aside from a few magic moments like the pelicans in Sandspit Park and the turkey vultures at St Lucie Docks and a few people who were friends here) I hated Florida, and I wanted out, as fast as we could. It took two years—and a long fact-finding trip up the east coast of the USA while we explored potential places where we could put down roots—he took me back to the town where he was born, to show me, and on the way we stopped off to stay with all our Misc.writing friends. We didn't find our home on that trip, but here's another moment, from it—on the way back, I somehow managed to catch a laryngitis from hell—sick as a dog, completely voiceless. We broke our journey in St Augustine which wasn't that far away from home, but we could go no further that evening. On a wretched night of sickness and suffering and a horrid fog that had come up outside—he found a hotel and tucked me into bed and then sailed out to get honey and tea for my wounded throat.

I barely had the voice to whisper a thank you. But always—always—I was priority number 1.

When I got married, my husband said to me, "You write. I'll deal with the mundane chores." And he did. He was the one who cooked (although we took turns taking out the garbage) and cleaned and did the laundry. He promised me a cup of coffee in bed every morning before I got up and he lived up to that promise every day except for a brief while when he physically could not carry a cup. And he also took over other things. He always was my first reader and my trusted editor, and that was an ongoing thing, a part of my writing process for all these years. Here's a Facebook post I made back in 2013–

6 August 2013

My husband in his role as my editor has definitely had an influence on me. Just now, writing, I wrote a line about "something very much like sardonic amusement"—and I clearly heard his voice behind me and he said "Weasel word!" And I said, "yes sir," and erased "something very much like". It was sardonic amusement, dammit. And I will state it categorically.

In the first two decades of the new millennium, we became partners in everything.

ↂ

BETWEEN 2000 AND 2020, I wrote and published 22 books of my own work and edited two anthologies—two million words in print, one way or another, with him, always, there as an entire one-man support system. During this time we shared triumphs and tragedies, award nominations and finalist placements, the publishing bloodbath of 2008 which lost me three editors and four publicists in quick succession and could have broken anyone—anyone else, that is, without Deck in their corner, sturdily supporting me through the thick and the thin, always proud of me, constantly handing out bookmarks featuring my books to anyone whom he happened to see reading on our travels while we went to various conventions and conferences during that period (he would continue to do this right to the end—he sold three books to various nurses from his hospital bed, during his last two months in a hospital bed). He would read all the words I put before him, and had the somewhat annoying but also oddly buoying habit of drawing a line along a page of prose with a single word ("fix") next to in in red pen, trusting me to know what to do in order to accomplish that. There were some hills I chose to die on to be sure but not that many—as an editor, he had a good eye for what needed "fixing" and the good sense to stay out of my way while I figured out how to do that. Writing became a whole process, and he was a huge part of it. I had a vague memory that I had once written on my own. This arrangement… seemed so much better. More productive. Somebody I trusted ALWAYS had my back.

He also dealt with my website. He created and constantly kept updated a Pinterest account in my name and worked hard at making it pull its weight and got frustrated when he couldn't make it do what he wanted—there would come a time, later, in the aftermath, that professionals would look at that jury rigged website held together by faith and hope and cyber-baling-wire, and would be bewildered how the whole thing had ever functioned at all (the magic glue was pure love). A non-techy, he learned whatever software he needed in order to make my life easier and softer—to let me live in my beautiful story dreams and create them in my reality. I only learned just how much he did when he was gone and I faced the lacuna—and there was so much, so much to do. He was with me for everything. All the way.

But… about that coffee, and the period in which he physically could not fulfil that promise that he had made.

℘

Let me go back to that last "special" year. 2003.

IN FEBRUARY OF 2003 WE finally shook the dust of Florida off our feet and moved into our home in Bellingham, Washington—a house surrounded by cedars, with deer and raccoons, and raucous jays and woodpeckers, and mourning doves, and hawks, and owls. We lived in that house for precisely four months, and in June of that year he was felled by a massive stroke.

From the ICU to a general hospital ward to a nursing home (to recover strength) to in-patient rehab, and then long-term out-patient rehab, I was with him all the way. Terrified, bewildered, anxious, but with him, all the way. I did not know how it would all play out—until I saw him, on my birthday, fight his way to his feet from the wheelchair he was in and stand up and take a first step—and I wept because I knew it was going to be all right after all. That he would never give up. That he would never surrender. That so long as we had each other everything else would be fine—that, in his own words, which I once threatened to carve into his tombstone, "nothing was insurmountable". He was left with a nearly dead right arm, and he walked with a cane but only when it came to uneven surfaces outside the home— here, in our haven in the woods, he moved slowly and carefully sometimes but there was nothing that would stop him. My coffee in bed resumed as soon as he could carry a cup in his good hand. He managed his own care and ablutions although I helped with things like putting on socks when he couldn't reach. I did what he needed. When he required help he would ask for it and would get it otherwise I did not get in his independent way. He still cooked every day. He made sure the coffee was always on. He made apple sauce, and he made cranberries from scratch on Thanksgiving and Christmas, and he enjoyed my baking forays when I (much later, in the pandemic year) started making bread, for instance.

Every year on the anniversary of his stroke I would give him a "rebirthday" card, marking the passage of these years, and every year was a gift. He made it to "happy 17ᵗʰ", but not #18. He didn't live to see that.

And honestly, I could go on for many thousands of words, but they would all come down to one simple single thing.

In the puzzle of each other's life, we were each the final and important piece, the one that completed the picture.

And then that important piece… well.

That is the rest of this story.

Losing

(Two and a Half Months

in Limbo)

The story of how I lost him… is one of those stories that has no beginning, actually. Because you go, "it started when…"—and then you think a little and go, "actually, no, it was before that, it started when…"—and it goes like that, step back by step back, until you are not at all sure where you are any more, a pile of puzzle pieces that belong somewhere in the center of the picture and some even link together in a coherent way but you've lost all track of the edges and you have no idea where all those blue pieces of sky are supposed to go.

So let's pick an arbitrary point of beginning.

The stroke happened in 2003. We survived it, and made a life around it. It wasn't perfect and it sometimes wasn't even easy but with each other to pick up slack where necessary and required we managed just fine.

Somewhere round about 2015—I'd tell you more precisely if I still had access to Deck's medical records, but they pulled his account post haste after he died, and I don't any more so we will just have to be a little nebulous about it—his doctor thought he heard a heart murmur. So he sent him to a cardiologist. The cardiologist gave him the wrong medication, one which exacerbates edema (from which Deck was already suffering)—I found that out when I did my research AFTER the fact. The direct result of this was that one morning his leg SLOSHED as he was lying in bed and I looked and there was the biggest goddamn blister I had ever seen in my life sitting there on his shin. I kid you not, this one single large blister was almost as big as my entire HAND, it covered the whole front of his shin. I don't need to tell you what gravity did to that thing when he tried to get out of bed—suffice it to say that it took some towels to mop it all up. And then we slapped some gauze on it.

And it went bad. It ulcerated—deep into the skin, into the fatty tissue beneath, you could SEE it. We went to the doctor, and the doctor sent him to the wound clinic where they treated such things. The treatment was agonizing (debridement of all the dead skin every time—which HURT—and a full lower leg mummy-like multilayer bandage which had to be kept dry and protected during ablutions—oh, it was miserable. But it healed, eventually. It left behind a large area of tight pink skin which was roughly the size and shape and position of the original blister—you could tell exactly where it had been. During the years that followed, occasional blisterlets would arise and then get gauzed (by me) and they would disappear again—this seemed to be something we would have to learn to expect—but mostly they were small, and innocuous enough, and they would come and go. It was endurable.

In November of 2020—the 9th, to be precise—I looked at his leg as he lay in bed and I just froze.

"It's back," I said. "The monster."

There was another blister. In almost exactly the same place that the original big one had been, and almost the same size.

"Maybe we should go see the doctor," I said.

"It'll be FINE," said my optimist husband. "Just stick some gauze on it if you have to. And put some honey on if you like." (We had already established—from my own family lore as a bee-keeper's granddaughter—that Honey Healed All…)

So we did that, on the 9th of November.

On the 10th, it was worse. On the 11th, it was worse still. I was losing this battle; changing his dressing often meant that I took the entire bloody upper layer with the gauze I was removing, which meant a lot of pus and ooze and blood, and I was starting to worry about maintaining the proper and necessary sterility.

On the 12th—and this was a new development—it began to hurt—not just to the touch but all the time—badly enough for it to be an issue. Deck resorted to Tylenol in order to be able to sleep. The next day was a Friday, and brought no improvement—and then, of course, it was the weekend. By Sunday the entire leg was swollen, red, and warm and a little puffy to the touch—and I began to have real fears of cellulitis.

The next day—November 16—was a Monday, and I managed to obtain an afternoon appointment with his doctor on an emergency basis.

His doctor looked at the leg and frowned. "You're right," he said, "it might well be potential cellulitis and it needs a strong dose of antibiotic, more than I can properly administer. Take him through to the ER and see what they think they need to do."

I burst into tears.

For months before this—MONTHS!—Deck had stayed at home while the specter of Covid raged through the land. The one place I did not want him anywhere near was the hospital ER, and its potential exposure to this deadly miasma that might be waiting there—who knew who else would be there and for what reason? But I was overruled. And so, sobbing, I took him to the ER of our local hospital.

They took off the makeshift dressing. They looked at the wound and frowned mightily. They took pictures. They took scans. They also started paying attention to an ancillary thing which was a large fissure in Deck's heel—his foot had "hurt" for a long time but we both thought it was something silly like his arches or plantar fasciitis or something of the sort but turned out he had a crack in his heel that was really difficult to see unless you crawled under his foot with a mirror—but suddenly that heel had to have No Pressure On It Whatsoever.

A conversation took place while we waited in the ER and it slowly got dark outside which, later, I was to recall with bitter clarity.

They said they were going to admit him to the hospital for at least overnight and one of the doctors said diffidently, "It's almost never an issue but we have to ask—in case of something dire happening like a cardiac arrest or anything life threatening do you want full code actions or is there a DNR?"

We said, don't keep him alive artificially. They said, ok.

He was admitted. They placed him (initially) on the cardiac ward—in a single-bed room with careful care and monitoring (and I was just glad he was OUT OF THE ER!) and I left him there at last, quite late that night, and went home.

They transferred him to a general ward the next day, and that was where I found him when I returned to see him. He was sitting in a chair, his wounded and bandaged leg out in front of him. We spoke to therapists, and to nurses, and on the day after that to at least one attending physician who voiced an opinion that Deck's presence there was something of an "overreaction", and that he probably shouldn't have been hospitalized at all (even though his own doctor sent him to the ER…) There's chatter of discharge on the 19th, but things aren't really improving at all, he is still on pain killers, the heel is now almost a bigger issue than the shin wound, and eventually we are told that they have found him a "swing bed" in a smaller facility out in Sedro Woolley, where he could recuperate and receive some physical and occupational therapy.

This happens on the 20th, and I have to reschedule the cats' annual vet visit to accommodate the necessities of this. I do not see him on this day (things are complex) because I do something wholly unrelated on the 20th—I go get my first post-covid haircut. I tell her that my husband says, "don't cut TOO much off…" (he loves my long hair…) but I am in constant touch by phone; I have access to his charts, and his meds, and I find out that he has been put back on the same heart medicine that gave him the initial blister in the first place so I raise Cain about that with the Sedro Woolley facility on the 21st and they say they will take him off those meds—but he is suddenly on a whole SLEW of medications, and yes, still on the antibiotics.

I have no real idea what happens next. I go to see him on the 22nd, and he's still on antibiotics, and still on painkillers. They tell me that they think he will be in that place for "at least a week". Probably through Thanksgiving.

We are in constant touch by phone. He's out of bed, and dressed now, and sitting in his armchair, which is an improvement, anyway. I take him clean clothes on the 23rd. On the 24th he reports he is having "lots of therapy"…

On November 26, Thanksgiving, I go to visit and for the first time I completely lose it, and weep copiously at a nurse. They tell me he is doing well, really well, and try to mop up the floods; he is still "doing well" on the 27th, when he reports to me on the phone that his occupational therapy person pronounced themselves really pleased with his progress. The wound is getting better—a lot better.

I'm still trying to finalise the Fractured Fairy Tales book which is due out in April of 2021, and there are still a few stories left to write. On Sunday, the 29th, I take one of the new stories to read to Deck—"Finley's Joy". He listens to me read it to him, and gives me that ultimate compliment that I treasured from him so much—"I hate you". He says the story is perfect. He says his friend the hospital chaplain is coming round to see him the next day, and can he keep the story to show her? (He is ALWAYS telling people about me, my writing, handing out bookmarks, selling my books to his nurses…) I say sure. That next day we have a phone conversation during which he reports that he has been told that it is entirely possible that he will be coming home in the first week of December. About time, say both of us. He has now been hospitalized for just about two whole weeks.

On December 1ˢᵗ, he has an appointment at the Wound Clinic in Bellingham, and the Sedro Woolley people ferry him there in their institutional van. I meet him there. The wound is progressing nicely, although he is still on intermittent painkillers which is a concern. The heel is not doing so well, but they're still trying to keep pressure off it (except Deck purely HATES the "pressure boot" they are trying to make him wear, because in order to be attached to his leg it straps across the front of his shin where the actual blister wound STILL IS and it hurts when they do that. This is now a conundrum. There are also hints at an actual release—Deck may finally be coming home. On December 8, they tell us. Well, December 8 or 9. Thereabouts.

On December 6, two things happen. I take "Glowstick Girl", the last fairy tale book story, in to show him (and again he wants to keep it, to show his chaplain friend). And then I come home. And have a complete meltdown, breaking down in tears. For no particular reason. Just because everything… has accumulated.

Or maybe I was prescient.

For the rest of this, I will use the reports I wrote up for the people following along on the Internet, in a series of Facebook posts.

Let me just say that everything up until now has been Purgatory.

On December 7, 2020, we finally push open the gates of Hell.

☙

7 December 2020

So, hubby is supposed to be coming home from nearly three weeks in various hospitals, this Wednesday. All plans are in process. Discharge. Transport. Home health visits when necessary. All of that.

I went to visit him in current hospital only yesterday.

Spent a couple of hours with him. He (as always) seemed in better spirits than me despite being the, yanno, actual patient.

This morning... I get a phone call from a "wireless caller". I usually don't even pick those up, let them go to voice mail, if I don't know the number I figure they can't want to talk to ME—but this time I pick up. And it's the doctor who is in charge of treating Hubs in the hospital there.

and what he had to say was...

"Your husband stopped breathing."

I dropped everything including the phone and probably broke speed records and/or the law at some point getting to the hospital. When I get there they had revived him, but he looked half dead, with blood on his mouth (they said they did CPR. Heavy duty CPR. They said it isn't uncommon for the patient to bite their lip or their tongue during that, hence the blood. But he looked like some species of vampire when I got there). He's on full mask oxygen. He's barely breathing right. When I first get there I don't think he was even aware I was there.

They brought him back, but his heart is now an issue. And where he is right now... is in the ICU unit in our main hospital.

My husband DIED this morning and then came back from the dead. And now he is in a place where the specter of the plague looms large.

He was supposed to come HOME. He was supposed to come home on Wednesday.

ॐ

8 December 2020

DECK UPDATE—he's still in the ICU but he is going to get transferred to a cardiac unit probably later today or tomorrow—I'm holding off going to see him until then because of several factors—I don't want to get underfoot in the ICU in general, but also it's the highest risk place and I have another high-risk person to take care of, my mom, and if I can avoid exposing myself to potential danger zones it's best for all concerned—so I'm waiting until he's moved to the cardiac unit, much quieter, with fewer people and less risk, and then I'll go over there to see him. But I spoke to him this morning and he sounded OK. They are, however, planning an angioplasty procedure as early as tomorrow (from what I've been able to gather).

Didn't get that much sleep last night, myself, and when I did drift off I kept jerking awake with an echo of that phone call in my head—"your husband has stopped breathing"—It is going to take me a week to get over yesterday. Also, for future reference for anyone who cares to keep a note of such things, driving on the highway in the twilight hour while in the grip of a full panic attack... is not advisable. The trucks had teeth.

UPDATED—see below

DECK SAYS to say to everybody that he deeply appreciates all the outpouring of good wishes and support. I swear, he's taking all this better than I am.

As best as I can piece it together (I still haven't spoken to an actual medical professional who can give me DETAILS) they appear to have found a blockage in an artery of his right leg and they're going in after that. they are also going to check the heart—In the same or a different procedure, I am not sure. But whatever is happening, it's happening tomorrow morning. Keep sending the good vibes.

I will know more tomorrow. Furthers and betters then, after they've had their rummage.

UPDATE:... they didn't do the procedure today. They'll do it tomorrow. I've been wound up tighter than a violin string all night and I kept pushing people off the phone because I was waiting for word from the hospital... only to hear that nothing has been done after all and won't be until tomorrow. I swear. I don't know how much more of this I can take...

☙

11 December 2020

UPDATE For those following at home.

Deck had an angiography procedure this morning. they found blockages. they put in FIVE STENTS...in one artery. They have to go back in, maybe in a day or two, to tackle the other one which the doctor described to me as a "more sophisticated" problem... which frankly is a phrase I hate hearing in a medical context....

He was in the recovery room for at least four or five hours after the procedure which I am told he "tolerated" well. there was anesthesia involved. they are now watching to see how his kidneys are tolerating the aggressive invasive stuff they had to pump him full of.

I haven't talked to him today. it wasn't possible. I feel like a wrung out dishrag.

That's where we are now. I have no idea how this ends. or when.

໑

12 December 2020

FURTHER UPDATES

"Garbo laughs"

Seriously I am not old enough to remember that when it was a "thing" but it was definitely a "Thing"— Garbo was famous for her melodramatic 'I vant to be alone' moments and when she was in a movie where she was called upon to laugh on screen that was a MOVIE PROMO LINE because they figured people would flock to see what Garbo looked like when she smiled.

Well, folks, I spent about half an hour on the phone with my hospital warrior this morning, and I swear, that man could find joy anywhere. Lying there in that bed feeling like a colander being fed medications like he was a turkey being fattened for Christmas... he found something to laugh about.

I love that man so much.

Looks like they're back in on Monday, attacking a second artery. and then possibly a third procedure to clear the leg vessels… and he is laughing.

He is LAUGHING.

I may be going in to see him tomorrow in the lull between the two procedures. I will let you all know if he is still laughing about all the things that life has thrown at him in the past three and a half weeks.

໑

13 December 2020

Quick update on The Situation—went to see Deck today, spent some time with him he's remarkably chipper given that he looks like a heavily bruised pin cushion with several IV ports and monitors hooked on and generally being in a situation that he is technically hogtied to his hospital bed with all the paraphernalia. I JUST missed his doctor, the cardiologist who performed his first angioplasty, but I was in time to observe the notes he left on the room information board—the second procedure, the one with the so-called "scrunched up" artery which they need to unobstruct, should be taking place tomorrow PM—with the help of a specialist in the "scrunching" that is in place. On the one hand glad that there will be a specialist in place on the other I'm gently freaking out that a specialist in attendance SEEMS TO BE INDICATED. That is all I know right now. But I held his poor bruised hand and did a dozen little loving things that the nurses don't have the time (or isn't in their job description) to do. I was there as they changed the dressing on his leg (it's almost astonishing how SECONDARY the thing that sent him to the hospital in the first place has become...) and that seems to be improving, under all the layers of gauze etc—they said the wound clinic nurse would be coming in to inspect tomorrow morning, so there's THAT to look forward to... And then I left him there again, to wait for the wound supervisor and the artery unscrunching.

Am back home, with two needy cats who really are NOT starving despite every indication that they are giving of the contrary, on my second cup of coffee, trying not to dwell on all the things that the dark bird-thoughts of my mind are fluttering around.

I'm looking around and realising that I probably

*need to water my plants, vacuum my house, catch up to
all the life and living that seems to have been slipping
under the radar of all of this... this... if I may borrow
and repurpose a word once used by Terry Pratchett, this
EMBUGGERANCE. I probably need to do... practical...
things tomorrow. It'll use up the day so that I don't spend it
thinking about what's going on back there in the hospital.*

*Oh, and I walked in there today and lifted a finger
and said solemnly to him, "I have a papercut. It hurts like
the blazes".*

*Tis true, but it was so deliberately ridiculous a
statement aimed at the man in that hospital bed that we
both fell about laughing. it felt good. It was worth the
paper slice, any day.*

ᘏᓀᓇ

14 December 2020

*I spoke too soon. I laughed too soon. [AA(comment):
they tried the second procedure. They punctured the artery
they were working on. Things are now suddenly very
WORSE...]*

ᘏᓀᓇ

16 December 2020

As The World Turns, the next exciting episode.

*So I had one important errand to run today—get that
second opinion (and a second quote) on the state and repair
of my ailing back brakes. So I went to a local iteration of
a large well known franchise, and they took the car for a
quick test drive and then came back and hoisted the poor
beast up high and off came its little round legs (I could*

see this through a window from the waiting area into the
workshops) And there it hangs, until the guy comes out
with a piece of metal in his hands.

The back brakes are semi shot, yes, But he says that is
NOT where the squealing noise that is driving me batty is
coming from, and he shows me the thing he is holding. It
is an important bit from the machinery that makes up the
FRONT brakes, and he points to a shiny spot where some
safety covering had worn quite away and the squealing
noise I was hearing was METAL GRINDING ON
METAL in the front brakes. Quite aside from annoying
this now assumes the mantle of downright unsafe. They
can fix it right now and right there—all four brakes—
and the GOOD news is that the price they quoted me
was considerably less than the one I originally had. (The
bad news is that it is not $$$ that I can readily part with
right now...) So I had it done, sat there and had it done
as I waited and watched, because all of a sudden *I was
literally afraid to get back in that car, especially in the
currently sluicing down rain*.

While I am sitting there I give mom a call because
I was going to be out of pocket for longer than I thought
I might be and she frets if she can't get hold of me when
she needs to (and for some reason she seems congenitally
incapable of dialling my cellphone number because she
swears she called but there is never a record of the call on
the phone). After establishing where I was and why (this is
a refrain. sigh. where are you? where are you going? when
are you going? when are you getting home? why are you
going? where exactly is the place you're going... street X...
oh, I don't know where that is... but where are you going?)
she leads with, "I have a problem."

There is a leak in her kitchen sink.

There is literally nothing I can do about that right then and there. Calling a plumber with "my mother says something is damp" is not going to hack it. I need to go there and see what is going on.

I am suddenly so very TIRED.

Earlier that morning I phoned the ICU to find out what the story was with Deck—and spoke to a nice male nurse who (bless him) is literally the slowest talker I have ever heard. I don't mean a drawl of an accent I just mean... that he... talks... very slowly... and it's like pulling teeth to find out anything relevant. But I did get out of him that they were still making final decisions on it but the drain that they had in him post the arterial puncture and the subsequent bleed is supposed to come out today, sometime today. And here I am stuck in the auto shop, waiting for brakes. I suppose I could have phoned again and bugged the living daylights out of them, but post brake job, with rain still pelting down and darkness closing in fast, I sit in the car and make a choice.

Go to mom's, establish the leak parameters, take steps.

Go to hospital, go see Deck, go see what is going on there.

Well, momma didn't mention a flood. Just "something damp". It will freaking keep.

I make tracks to the hospital.

I swear to you I never knew there were so many tubes and wires that could go into a single human body. but for a man who's been to hell and back he looks pretty good. well bruised, like he's been in a fight with an entire antagonistically inclined thug gang, and wired up like a marionette, but he smiles when he sees me. And I know I made the right choice.

He tells me they told him a bit more about the whole situation. They have done tests and scans and oh la la god knows what and the upshot knock wood very hard is that he was told that the heart was "good". They already fixed the one artery, the one with the five stents now in it, and apparently the blockage in the second one although not cleared has been found a way around, so to speak. They're still monitoring his... his... well, they're monitoring everything... but the ICU nurse (the slowspoken one I talked to before—same guy) thinks that the major sensors can come off tomorrow if tonight goes according to parameters.

I sat there holding his hand and he clutched at mine and the nurses probably thought we were something quite odd. He asked me to stay until they brought him dinner and so I did, and because he's so wired up and they brought soup I helped him eat it without making a major mess of the bed.

Oh and the wound that sent him there in the first place? So far it's been bundled up in layers of medication and gauze. right now? It's got a single large band aid on it. I suppose that says something.

It's been another DAY and I'm tired out for no particular reason. But that brake bit with the protective material worn through and the bare metal scraping until it is sharp and shiny...? that is an oddly appropriate metaphor for me right now.

Well. I replaced the brakes. I was told I need new tires, too, but that's a saga for another day. I crawled back home again, fed the indignant cats ("where the hell WERE you all day do you know it's dark outside and we're starving???")

and now I am about to go make myself a cup of coffee and fall over.

Tomorrow is another day.

୧୨

18 December 2020

State of play.

Cats had to go to their annual exam yesterday and a kind neighbor volunteered to ferry them there and back. My little boy decided that this would be a fine time to poop in his carrier, and then, at the vet's, further disgraced himself by escaping from the examination room and causing three veterinary assistants to chase, corner, and retrieve him forthwith. The good news is that he seems to have recovered well from this summer's urinary blockage episode (knock wood). My dowager queen cat, however, got a "callback" because the vet has noticed a new heart murmur and her blood pressure is rather high (the cat appears to have been rather entirely too empathetic with what is happening to the currently hospitalized "parent"...) so I need to take her back for another look in January (weather permitting)

My Jewish neighbor lady for whom I make challah bread decided, in the spirit of Chanukah, to deliver a pile of latkes to my door. They are... rather good. She delivered them in two batches, one to eat now (for me) and one to freeze ("for when your husband gets home") So I cried over that. A little.

The husband. Oh, oh, oh, the husband.

Reader, he is now a cyborg. They put in a pacemaker. This changes the picture again.

He is still in the ICU but the major monitors have been taken off now and he is technically waiting for a bed (again...) to be transferred up into the cardiac ward.

I spoke to a nurse this morning who hammered me all over again saying that there has been a referral to "palliative care". To me, that means end-of-life stuff, when medicine washes its hands of you; the nurse insists that's a "common misconception, either way that is a meeting to be had in the coming week. It was another semantic shock and when I put the phone down from THAT I cried again. I seem to cry easily these days, it doesn't take much to set me off, and now I'm scared all over again—because what happens when he does come home? The pacemaker now means that he is a serious SERIOUS heart patient and how am I supposed to be able to take care of him? How can he come home? Is he ever coming home? How does this all end? I spoke to himself, briefly, in the afternoon—but the phone in that place gives him a lot of trouble and our conversations are always rather brief. He had trenchant opinions on the person who told me about the palliative care thing - and he had been spoken to about it too—and insists that he is, he IS, coming home. But I'm still sitting here shaking all over again. I don't know how this ends, where this ends, and how much it is still going to extract from him and from me—but one of the questions that we are supposed to be discussing with the palliative care people is whether everything he has been through in the last couple of weeks has been "Worth it"... I mean... as opposed to what? having let him stay dead when he first had the cardiac episode? I'm shaken up and upset all over again. I am going in to see him tomorrow, but I dare say none of the necessary conversations will be had before Monday at the earliest which gives me the whole entire weekend to fret

*about it. Was it "worth" it? Is every minute of every day of
a world with him in it "worth " it? Is it?...*

*Anyone wants to talk me down from the ledge, have
at it. I have made more typos in this post than I have in
anything in a long time. [AA note: corrected for the purpose
of not shaming myself in a proper publication…] I am
forgetting how to think straight.*

❧

20 December 2020

*So I wrote a little something - it's called "Of ransom,
and time travel". Much of it will be familiar to many
of you. My apologies for rehashing stuff. I was just
refocusing...*

It's five days to Christmas.

Let me bring you up to speed (again)

*So, on November 16 my husband picked up his trusty
cane and made his careful way to the car so that we could
go visit his doctor to see about a wound in his leg that
wasn't healing—that had, in fact, been going steadily worse
and worse over the course of four or five days and was
now well into the stage of probable infection and possible
cellulitis. The doctor sent him to the ER. The ER people
admitted him to the hospital for a mega dose of intravenous
antibiotic.*

*After four days in the Big Hospital they transferred
him to a smaller place, a rural hospital in a nearby small
town with some 23 or so inpatient beds, where he could
receive some physical therapy to, so to speak, put him back
on his feet. Sometime during this transfer, the cane which I
mentioned earlier simply disappeared. I know it was in his*

hospital room in the Big Hospital because I saw it there; it was NOT in his room in the Little Hospital when I went THERE to see him the next day. A few perfunctory phone calls were made but the cane was GONE. Vanished.

It had history. It was one I bought him when he first returned from the brink after the stroke of 2003. It might have been a Christmas gift that year, even, not sure now. It was a nice wooden cane, walnut maybe, and by now it was carrying seventeen years of scars and memories. It had carried and supported him all that time and all I can say is, its disappearance gave me a pang. "It's only a cane", my husband said, "although I did treasure it because you gave it to me." But he felt it too—it was a tangible symbol of seventeen years which were sometimes not easy ones. But it was gone.

He spent the next little while in the Little Hospital, recuperating, it seemed, nicely. It was as though the system took the cane as ransom and gave back a recovery period which seemed to lead to him coming home on December 9—everything was in place for that.

On December 6, a Sunday, I went to visit him at the Little Hospital. I took a new story to show him. He was bright, alert, steady as always, things were going to be a little tough for a little while but we'd faced worse, he was coming home on the Wednesday, it was all set and sorted.

On the morning of December 7th, the ransom ran out.

I usually don't even pick up the phone when the caller ID feature just says "wireless caller" because it's usually a robocall trying to either scam me or sell me something. But this time I pick up the phone and I get the doctor taking care of him at the hospital. He says to me, "your husband stopped breathing."

So did I.

I don't know how I got there and it is a miracle I did not hit anything on the way but by the time I arrived at the hospital he was—post vicious but necessary CPR that left him with an agonizingly painful chest—coming back to himself, a little. But there was nothing the little hospital could do for him at this point. He was turfed back into an ambulance, and back to the Big Hospital he came, this time to the ICU. He was attached to various IVs and wires and monitors, and they stabilized him. He had an angioplasty procedure which opened up one blocked artery. They moved him out of the ICU onto the cardiac ward some three or so days later, when a bed opened up, and back I went to see him, a couple of times.

The last time I went to see him, it was on another Sunday, the 13th—and I sat with him for a couple of hours. Again, he was awake, alert, chipper, we laughed together at silly things. The second angiography procedure, for a second blocked artery, was up on the board in his room for that Monday at 3 pm.

They took him into the procedure on Monday morning instead.

When the phone call from that doctor came, I knew immediately something awful had gone wrong—when they lead with things that CAN happen you somehow know that they are going to end up with "well that did happen". The second artery's blockage was more extensive, they tried to go around it, and they punctured the artery in the process. There was bleeding in the pericardial sac, and now there was a drain in his chest to make sure that didn't accumulate. He spent Monday unconscious and intubated. It was only on Tuesday that he swam back to consciousness, and he spent the next few days in the ICU hooked up to everything in creation again. They inserted a pacemaker. They took him back up into a room on the cardiac ward five days later… and at some point I realized that the hospital had taken another ransom, another tithe. My favourite hat was missing—a hat I last saw in the hospital, visiting him.

Cane. Payment for cardiac arrest resuscitation, for a successful first angioplasty.

Hat. For returning him from the brink of that second procedure.

I don't know how many lives he has left, or what I can offer in exchange for a gift of them. My life has become a pagan ritual, offering sacrifices for boons, whispering "don't leave me alone" while wrapped in dark solitary midnights, sitting in my living room and cupping my two hands over air as though I was holding his own phantom hand there and whispering "stay with me". I wonder what is the next thing that will be demanded.

In other news, I did cyber-enhanced time travel this morning. By the power vested in all of us by the magical internet, a Zoom meeting was set up—between me and a school friend whom I met when we were fifteen years old and whom I last saw in person it must have been thirty years ago now (I know. I am emphatically not old enough to have known anyone for that long…) She brought in another school friend of the same era. We talked about setting up another meeting for Christmas, with all of us in various forms of lockdown in the plague era. Grown women, senior women, even, coming together… after forty years… it was time travel. It took me back to a different age. An age where all I had to worry about was passing my O Levels, and nobody was sick, and nobody was dying, and the world didn't have the plague, and everything (from today's perspective at least) was gentle and serene and sane.

I miss that. I do.

I'll go back to preparing pagan sacrifices now. I had a definite Christmas Carol moment there—days of Christmas Past (with all the schooltime connections), Christmas Present (dealing with situations in the here and now, like husband's heart issues, elderly mother issues, fixing the car issues…), and Christmas Future, wondering what the next thing I need to offer up on the altar might be, for everything to be okay.

In a handful of days it is going to be a whole new year, and we are officially moving into the third decade of the twenty first century. I never knew the future would be so perilous, back when my friends and I were schoolgirls together.

I wonder what lies waiting round the bend.

☙

23 December 2020

The Department of "The center cannot hold"…

Short one right now because I'm about to crack up, I swear I am.

They're turfing Deck out of the hospital because there isn't anything further that they can MEDICALLY do at this point and he's taking up a hospital bed and I can see their point, I CAN, but this arrangement meant that I could rock up at the hospital, have my temperature taken, and be allowed in to see him at whatever point. And we could sit and talk and hold hands and whatever. It was a lifeline.

There's "no room" at the little rural hospital he was at before, so they're turfing him into a "short term rehab center", aka a freaking NURSING HOME which is exactly and precisely where I do not want him at all—and I just got off the phone with *them*.

They're quarantining him for fourteen days. No outside contact. No visitors at all (they can "Arrange Facetime video calls with friends and family"...). But no physical contact, no physical visitors, and even after the 14 days (if he is there for that long) he may only be moved into a different room which allows for "window visits" with people.

This was our lifeline. THIS WAS OUR LIFELINE. The fact that we were there for one another.

This isn't going to work. it isn't going to work. It will kill us both.

He's on his way there now. We'll see how it goes for a day or two but if this is a new reality then I don't care what happens or what I have to do... I'm bringing him home. *I'M BRINGING HIM HOME*. They can provide home health help, and we will make do with that. But this... this is not going to work.

My head feels like it's in a vise. I'm in a Harlan Ellison story - I have no mouth and I must scream...

൚

26 December 2020

This pathetic little photo? It's the pile of Christmas

*presents. Untouched. it's the day after Christmas. and I'm
very rapidly reaching the stage of bah, humbug. But let me
bring you up to speed.*

*They discharged Deck from hospital. Or at least
they kicked him out which is closer to the truth. NO
discharge planning, NO meeting with anyone who could
tell me what comes next (as primary caregiver for a new
pacemaker patient—they handed him a gadget at some
point, with no further instructions than pictionary stuff
that came in the box, it's some sort of heart monitor. How
is it supposed to be used? When? How often? who gets the
data or how do I get the data to whoever needs to have it?).
He's on a slew of new meds—am I supposed to do my own
research on these? Nobody told me what they are, what
they are for, if they are permanent, or any other pertinent
details at all. He was supposedly referred to a palliative
care team—so far as I know, he was visited by a couple of
people (they came in together and talked to him some, but
from what I can gather it wasn't an in-depth visit of any
sort) before they turfed him out—was that it, for palliative
care? Does he have a contact in hospital for this? is there a
referral to someone else? I was told nothing, contacted by
nobody at all.*

*After I said to six different people NO NURSING
HOMES... I was more or less told that he was being taken
to one, on the 23rd of December, again, no consultation,
no alternatives, nothing—where he was supposed to get
"intensive rehabilitation and therapy". His insurance for
this kind of thing runs out tomorrow. His new insurance
plan doesn't kick in until January 1. Not sure what is
supposed to happen here—but let me just say several things.
1) they put a high risk patient into a nursing home which
is where the Covid madness started over here—but ok, let's*

say it was for intensive therapy; 2) he was parked there on the afternoon of the 23rd, and told "see you tomorrow"; he was spoken to by a random person or two on the 24th and nobody at all on the 25th (because CHRISTMAS) and so far as I can tell he has had a sum total of maybe three hours of desultory "therapy" since he got there and the rest of the time he was just left lying in his bed. He is under a 14-day quarantine—even though he was tested for Covid in the hospital every couple of days and was negative every time—but until this quarantine period is over HE IS NOT PERMITTED OUTSIDE HIS ROOM—I thought the whole idea of "intensive therapy" was the fact that this was a rehab facility that has the gym necessary for such things but he isn't even allowed near the gym for two weeks, apparently. So I am not at all sure why he was taken there in the first place. The 14 day quarantine also means the enforced separation which meant that we spent Christmas apart—and it was only through the agencies of a nurse who 'lent' us her phone that we were able to do a Zoom call yesterday. On Christmas day—they sequester people from everything—but they can't even make a plan for a patient to say Merry Christmas to someone they love?

I've been leaving messages for everyone, but nobody is at their desks. Because, yanno, Christmas. Holidays. You'd think the world just stopped, wouldn't you? All medical and other emergencies simply stop existing, do they, because it's "Christmas" and everyone's off duty? Could they not put on a reachable emergency staff of some sort, even if they have to pull short straws? I know it sucks, but hey, people, it sucks for people who AREN'T having Christmas too, and it sucks far worse. I can tell you that leaving messages for people who are going to be "back in the office" in five days' time is soul numbing. Maybe they have that kind of time. I don't.

My husband is stuck alone in a hospital bed without even the rehab therapy he is supposed to be there for (I was there today to leave him a card—I asked to speak to anyone on the therapy team, and was told that they had "gone home". This was at one PM-ish. this means that he is getting no therapy today, either. And tomorrow is Sunday, so you know, SUNDAY. They put him into solitary confinement for FIVE DAYS FOR NO REASON AT ALL. He could have come home and had home health visits, for this. He could have been home. If therapy was indicated they could have kept him in the hospital for two more days until the "holidays" were over and where he could have been paid more attention to.

He hates it there, and there doesn't seem to be any earthly reason why he is there in the first place, and they're going to send US the bill for this, I am helpless, and frustrated, and ANGRY, and clawing at shadows.

And that pile of unopened Christmas presents is a wound on my soul.

❧

27 December 2020

Couple of things.

You people are wonderful (thank you for the brownies, Susan).

Thank you for the support. Thank you for the 1 AM phone calls, those of you who were there for those. Thank you for being there.

Also, I FINALLY GOT HOLD OF SOMEBODY today. And there is going to be a long-overdue phone care conference tomorrow after which the path forward is going to be much clearer.

Also, I just put the phone down with His Nibs In Seclusion—and after nearly a week of nothing happening and him being locked into his hospital bed today they were finally doing something therapeutic with him. It wasn't much in itself but to him it was monumental because *something is happening at last* and we can talk about what happens next now, tomorrow at that conference call.

But I still have some phone calls to make, tomorrow. The hospital still needs dealing with.

I might, however, sleep a little better today.

Again.

Thank you. ALL of you.

❧

31 December 2020 11:47 AM

One tiny victory at a time (but I have to fight for everything...) They swopped him out of his inner-keep-walled-in-cask-of-amontillado room for the window room but it came with a price—there was a chair in the new room, yes, but Deck described it as "hard as a rock" and it was impossible to sit in for a long time because it was acutely uncomfortable for him. In the other room, he said he slept in the chair that was there at least once, and it was cushioned enough to be comfortable for that. I asked if he'd asked anyone if they could swap out the chairs or at least get extra cushioning and he said that yes, he did, four times, but the hard chair was still there in its unchanged form. So I called the guy whose name I had on record as caring for him, on the nursing staff, and outlined the problem, and asked if he could have the other chair in his new room—and if not if they could at least put pillows under his rear when they sat him up there.

Upshot? just got a call back. They swapped the chairs out and he has his comfy chair back now. It's something.

On the downside, his blood is still too thin for him to have therapy but worse, for me, is the fact that they have literally discontinued the blood thinners for now and the high numbers aren't coming down. And they won't give him any more therapy of any sort until those numbers have literally halved. They don't want to do things artificially because giving him things to "thicken" his blood puts him at risk for Bad Stuff and of course I don't want that and neither does he. But I am concerned about the numbers staying so high for so long.

But at least he can sit in a comfortable chair now.

One thing at a time.

I asked him if he wanted me to sit outside his window at midnight drinking a bottle of wine and miming "happy new year" at him. I think the facility might take a dim view of that though.

31 December 2020, afternoon

I just paid a couple of bills, writing checks to be mailed tomorrow (yes I still mail checks. I'm an old fogey. sue me.). I cannot BEGIN to tell you how wonderful it was to write "2021" on those checks. You know how people are always lagging behind when it comes to things like this automatically dating stuff with the year just over? I don't think we're going to have that problem, somehow, this year. Everyone is just too hyper aware of those wretched numbers.

UPDATE and speaking of bills... they're starting... just got two doctors bills today. One of them is inexplicably for five dollars. FIVE. I am not certain how they calculate those things. The other is... considerably more than that...

I went out into a rainy twilight as the last night of the old year drew in, and went to a cellphone place, and got a phone and a short term contract for Himself locked away in his cell there like a princess guarded by a horde of dragons, and then delivered it to the nursing home, I gave it to a nice young man and asked him to help Deck manage to figure it out—we exchanged a few words on the new phone but it needs to be plugged in to charge before anything more can be done with it. I got to tell him happy new year, and I saw him ensconced in his comfy chair, and I suppose that's all I can hope for right now. In a few more hours I'll ring in the new year, alone. And hope that it brings him home to me. soon. soon. soon.

(They tell me they're giving him vitamin K now, to try and gently and slowly bring down those skyrocketing blood thinner numbers. The way it was explained to me partially was that it's like eating a lot of broccoli. Now I have an insane urge to go deliver a metric tonne of broccoli to the nursing home doors and insist that they feed him it... but what I did instead is send a message to his own primary care physician's office making sure *he* knows what's going on over there right now. It's as good as a pile of broccoli to know that they know that oversight is being had...)

ৎৎ

2 January 2021

quick update to the update.

On this BITCH of a night, someone actually came out there to do an evaluation on Deck, just now (literally maybe half an hour ago). We didn't get very far—but we knew that, even the progress he was making three days ago was THREE DAYS AGO and he's been pretty much flat on his back since then, again. one step forward two steps back, as it were. But at least someone was THERE, and it's progress.

I'm not asking them to get him ready for a track meet. Really. All he wants to do is to be able to get cleared for literally standing up without howling for a pack of sled dogs to drag him up, and to be able to walk a dozen steps from here to there which would enable him to choose whether he wants a bed or a chair, or a bathroom by himself. That's my low-enough hanging fruit for now. if he can do THAT he can come home.

He can come home.

We have lived with limited mobility here in the house for eighteen years. we know how. But we need that mobility—however limited—built back up and god knows that isn't going to happen with no rehab at all. So anything is good. I'm grateful someone came to see him tonight. It gives me hope for tomorrow.

Warning—DeckUpdate—scroll on by if you can't bear the sight of these any more—they're cathartic for me so I keep on scribbling them...

Let's see where did we leave off? Let's do a QUICK recap because I want to do a totting up.

Admitted to facility he is in now on Dec 23 for "intensive therapy and rehab". On admission day, seen in passing while they said "welcome to your bed".

Dec24/25—an hour of "therapy" which consisted mostly of helping him stand up on his own two feet, nothing more strenuous than that.

Dec 26, not sure, but on Dec 27 we had the healthcare "conference" where nurses and therapists, oh my, all weighed in on the phone (remember, I am not allowed in there at all). It is made VERY clear that the priority is intensive therapy so that he can COME HOME as soon as possible.

December 28 or 29—his bloodwork goes kablooey (the values they measure were literally four times what they should have been) his blood is now thinner than water. The blood thinner drugs that he has been on and supposedly HAS to be on are discontinued for the nonce; more than that, he is given vitamin K to THICKEN the blood now. He had had no therapy of any sort because they were too afraid of the possibility of injury and of a "fatal bleed" (their words)—but on Dec 30 with all this still in play he is considered fine enough to be taken out of his bed, into a wheelchair, into a van, into an outside doctor's office (the wound therapy place, no less, with the possibility of blood-drawing abridement of the wound, but the thin blood question doesn't seem to arise...), out of the wheelchair and onto an examination table, and then the reverse—but no therapy. No assistance to even stay standing for five minutes. And he is basically ordered into bed when his dayshift nurse ends her shift so he's even taken out of the chair in which he is sitting so that he can be locked into bed again.

No therapy (he is basically being left to rot there) on Dec 29, 30, 31, Jan 1. Today, I phone the facility.

Oh, they don't have the requisite staff there today. (it's the WEEKEND, right...?) Maybe someone can "evaluate" him tomorrow.

Always assuming his bloodwork numbers are "good

enough" for someone not to have to take CYA action over it.

He was sent to a rehab facility for INTENSIVE THERAPY AND REHABILITATION and so far he has had maybe a sum total of four or five hours of anything that can be called by that name since DECEMBER 23. Because Christmas. Because New Year's. Because WEEKEND. I don't know, because something. And yes, I appreciate that staff work damn hard and they need time off too. But there are no shifts? Do they have people who work there who might not "keep" Christmas and who might have a therapy shift available to give? I mean, they are medical personnel. If he and I are aware of the fact that the more time he spends in bed or in a chair or immobile the worse his odds become—why aren't they? Why aren't extra efforts made, over the holidays/weekends? Do patients cease to exist during those times? I know I am demanding something here but it is no less than what he has been sent there to receive. If they were unable to offer that why accept the patient at all? these people didn't ask to be there "over the holidays" and they have no choice at all—do they deserve being left until things are more convenient?...

I just sent an email to the social worker in charge of his case. I am debating whether to phone the facility again and ask if I can pay for a therapist to come in, on overtime, and work with him for at least an hour. Anything. ANYTHING. he is a fighter, but I don't know how long he can stay one in the face of a brick wall— HE IS THERE TO GET REHAB AND HE IS NOT GETTING REHAB (because everyone has better things to do, apparently).

It was made very clear—to multiple people, multiple times—that he should be there for as short a time as possible. Every hour that they leave him to his own devices prolongs that period. And tomorrow of course is SUNDAY so—probably—nothing doing until Monday morning. They are stealing days from us. They are stealing a part of life which we could have shared. And it wouldn't maybe even be so hard if I could see that something was being done to shorten this period. But all I'm getting is Alice's Tea Party. Therapy yesterday and therapy tomorrow but never therapy today.

He's frustrated and upset. I'm frustrated and angry. but he is in their power, and I need to be quiet and calm and gentle and polite.

Oh dear god. Help me Obi-wan Kenobi you're our only hope...

ↄ৲

3 January 2021

quick update to the quick update to the previous update—someone actually came in and worked with Deck this morning as in PT therapy—they (rightly) aren't making him do the impossible but they are working on the POSSIBLE, at last, and both he and I are happier for it. Just spoke to him (on his new cellphone on which he can't find anything and I'm not there to show him and if I were he wouldn't need it so SIGH) and while he is still chair-bound and semi-frustrated SOMETHING IS HAPPENING and he sounds the happier for it.

Baby steps. literally. baby steps.

I prepared the coffeemaker last night for use this morning... except... that this morning I turned it on and discovered I had omitted a very important part of the process. As in, putting the actual coffee in the hopper. So when I turned it on this morning I got a cup of... hot water.

Sigh.

I rectified the situation but it took some doing and another disaster in its wake (I'd put in a muffin to toast— and then the coffee thing happened, or didn't happen, as it were—and I forgot the muffin and it burned and there was smoke and the smoke alarm went off and the cats went kablooey until I could get the screaming noise cut off...) but I finally have coffee...

❧

5 January 2021

oh-KAY, then. updaaaaate.

They're being very, very, very extra special very careful and pacemaker and heart and all that—and he is not supposed to lift or push more than 10 pounds with his left hand/arm without a bless-you-my-son release from his cardiologist (and THAT appointment isn't until the end of the month, oyvey) and you have to remember that his right side doesn't work all that well post stroke so his left arm IS what he uses to push off of stuff so there are ISSUES here... but today the therapy people came and he finally got stood on his hind legs again after GOD knows how long in beds and chairs. They wouldn't let him take a step—and he frankly says that he's just as happy about that RIGHT NOW—but at least he got vertical again. This is progress. If we can get this happening on a regular basis—followed by the ability to TAKE those few steps necessary to cross a room between a chair and the bathroom to do the necessary there instead of having to cope with make-do solutions dictated by being effectively confined to bed—and that's when we can come home, with any further therapy being done by home care, right here.

But they stood him up today. And so I stood up and cheered, in solidarity, before sitting back down to write this post.

From standing no-step to one step at a time. we're on our way.

Quickie post update—just finished talking with him—he says that what they want to try working with next (once they're happy with JUST STANDING) is transfers—bed to chair, chair to bed. THAT will be HUGE. After that, hopefully, the Grand Trek To The Bathroom And Back. We don't need him to be able to go on hikes. but being self-ambulatory to go where he wants to go when he wants to go there... that's the holy grail right now...

༖

7 January 2021

Okay ladies and gentlemen this is kind of a BIG bite.

I've watched friends talk about themselves or their friends or family who caught the bug. Some recovered, and some did not. I have watched friends who are in the front lines, like nurses, who have been battling this from the beginning, and watched them get more and more tired but stay defiant, and hoped that their impossible hours and unbearable working conditions would not grind them under or expose THEM to the deadly thing.

But up until now, I and mine have been skulking in the shadows—some in damn near solitary confinement (my mom, and Deck before this all happened and certainly since then in major ways, have been in confinement because of Covid because they are both in the highly vulnerable demographic) and others, a.k.a. me, only going out where and when I absolutely have to, masked up the wazoo, trying not to breathe too hard. I've been sheltering the people I love as best I knew how, and trying to stay out of sight as I did so, trying not to become a moving target myself.

We all just turned and looked covid in the eye.

Deck called me less than an hour ago.

He's had the first shot of the vaccine.

Hell just got a lot more real, folks. That spectre I was fighting so hard to keep outside the door of my home, my haven, my castle... it's now in the room with me. Admittedly it's in a good way—we hope—because the vaccine means that we can at least hope that the plague will pass us by. But still. It's a cold and clammy ghost that just breathed softly down the back of my neck.

I admit. I'm a little shaken. Relieved maybe—at some point—but right now, shaken.

I've NEVER been this close before.

ↁ

10 January 2021

Further developments.

Deck's blood numbers—the ones that preclude therapy—are up again and all that I'm getting from them is that they're "monitoring" this. That's fine. WHAT IS CAUSING THIS? Is anyone on that job? And the numbers were down to 5—which is the upper maximum they will permit for therapy—and someone came in and said to Deck, oh, high number, no therapy today. I just spoke to his nurse. The nurse said to me, "sometimes he refuses therapy". This man, who is frustrated to the max by sitting in the chair all day doing nothing, who hates being put into what he calls his "prison bed" every night, refuses therapy? HE IS BEGGING FOR THERAPY. And quite honestly I trust him more than I trust anyone else at this point. He is not mentally incompetent, and he would not lie to me. When he doesn't get therapy is when he isn't offered any, not when he "Refuses" it.

It is of COURSE Sunday. I left messages and emails and whatever I could with anyone I could think of. But I'm getting increasingly concerned with what is being done here and it is partly due to his physical disability at this point and partly due to what this is doing to his psychological state of mind. he needs something to work towards (getting home) and getting therapy is the primary thing that will accomplish tha—but I am not liking what I am hearing here, not at all.

He hasn't had therapy for—oh, I think this is the second day, again, today. The man who greets me in the morning when I phone him with "it's a bad day, no therapy" is not a man who is refusing therapy when it is being offered. I think I am inching closer to a full-on patient advocate here. I am thinking I am not being told the whole truth, and I am not liking it.

❧

11 January 2021

UPDATE—I left messages and emails for

EVVVVERYBODY. This morning they called me up and asked if I was available at 12 noon for another care conference. You can bet I have a list of questions in front of me. More later.

UPDATE TO THE UPDATE

They've consulted a cardiologist and are changing his meds to stabilise his blood numbers. I have put the "refused therapy" nurse person on record with the care manager at the place (who said he would investigate the thing—I don't know whether or not he ends up doing it but there's a record of it now and that phrase might be harder to invoke from now on). Therapy has undertaken to incrementally increase work with him and have given him exercises to do to strengthen relevant muscles when they aren't working with him. They're talking about "pacemaker restrictions" and that they're constrained with those right now and they can only be lifted by his cardiologist whom he doesn't see until the 29th and I'm trying to move that appointment up to an earlier date if I can (he's currently on waitlist for that) We have both underlined that the idea is to push forward—with every regard to safety issues— as hard as possible with an idea to coming home ASAP. And I demanded they set up another conference for next week. I WILL be kept in this loop, and I WILL be there to have Deck's back in whatever decisions he makes and wants implemented in the context. He hadn't had therapy yet before the conference, but he was going to get some immediately after. I'll call him later to see how it went.

He's going to the wound clinic for another appointment on Wednesday and I hope THEY can deal with the heel issue better there.

That's where we are folks. We have to see what the new

meds do.

His poor battered carcass just needs to keep hanging in there....and strengthen its muscles.

ༀ

13 January 2021

Deck's a tired puppy today but that's GOOD. Really. it's absolutely tremendous. They actually took him out of his room and more than ten steps away from his bed, as it were, for perhaps the first time since he got to the place he's in (not counting the doctor appointments and such...) and they introduced him to the rehab gym they have there. He said they tried a 90-degree turn—with the aid of the parallel bars—and then they even tried him on a paddling machine for a vanishingly short moment of time, but they tried him on it. He says his legs hurt in the BEST way.

But I do think that FOR ONCE he was glad to be back in the comfy armchair, for the nonce.

Me, I'm positively GIDDY.

ༀ

15 January 2021

So I crept out of my house today—to go make funny faces at Deck through his window while he desperately tries to find the right button to push on the cellphone (the man hasn't mastered the swipe. good thing he doesn't do online dating...) and then, on the way home I slipped briefly into the Whatcom Falls park because after the rains the falls had to be ROARING. They were; I took photos with my phone (deck struggles with swiping I go out and make waterfall videos HAH)... and then...

This group of young people comes across the bridge, while I'm standing there taking my picture. I mean. I AM STANDING THERE, already, stationary, clearly engaged in an activity. They...

Social distancing? what social distancing? Three or four of them come right up to where I was and casually lean on the bridge railing—at least two of them are wearing no mask at all, another is wearing it on his chin (why are people that stupid?). I back away, turning around to glare daggers at them. At least one of the maskless wonders has the grace to look guilty and kind of pushes off the railing and removes himself but at least two of the others are utterly oblivious. Kids, you may think you're immortal and you may be but STAY THE HELL AWAY FROM ME if you aren't prepared to do the most minor concessions in order to prevent the spread of this embuggerance.

Also, here's a moment of mental dissonance from the outing that will make you laugh. I see, in front of me, a young woman crossing the path pushing a blue baby buggy... or at least that's what I THOUGHT I saw... right until the moment she, under my shocked and horrified gaze until I did my double take, upended the "baby buggy", which was in fact a blue wheelbarrow filled with detritus from the storm of the other day, into the underbrush on the other side of the path. For a moment there it really looked like I was witnessing a fed up mother just upending her infant into the ferns, there...

☙

17 January 2021

Drive-by update for those following along at home.

Somehow or other my beloved has managed to do something to his new cellphone which makes it NOT RING when I call him. Last night I nearly lost my mind trying to get through to him and finally called the institution and got a nurse or somebody to go over there and tell him to CALL ME. Apparently someone futzed with the phone trying to get WiFi turned on and I don't know what they did but now it just doesn't ring and goes straight to voice mail and I told him to FIX IT and FIX IT NOW and he contritely said yes ma'am but I don't know how he's going to do it. His favourite therapist—a speech therapist whom he actually likes and who seems to be reasonably tech savvy—is coming tomorrow, he says, and he can ask her. But in the meantime... grrr.

On the therapy front, he had rehab this morning, he did the transfer between his armchair and the wheelchair himself, they took him to the gym again and he says he spent nearly a quarter of an hour on the bicycle machine (how they get him on and off that that thing I don't dare ask) and when he came back to his room he was "knackered" but it is moving in the right direction.

They're waiting for the damned sign-off from the heart doctor to allow him to do things like a more strenuous pull and that could mean the addition of a grab bar which would allow him more mobility but that isn't happening until at least the 29th (which is when his cardiologist appointment is). In the meantime, yesterday marked the second monthiversary of his going into hospital. This is getting surreal.

And now, if you will all excuse me, I need to go excavate my desk. There is something I need to find and I think it may be buried under piles of forms, letters, slips of paper with phone numbers of various doctors and hospitals, and general medical mayhem. My desk is a real metaphor for my life right now—just BURIED under medical adminstrivia...

၄၅

22 January 2021

Update on the Deckiverse, from the man himself. This photo was taken through the window tonight at about 5 pm-ish, and we have the following to report.

Next week is going to be BUSY because he is supposed to have no less than THREE different doctor appointments. But they may be a titch more bearable because...

...today he transferred between chair and wheelchair himself under his own steam and they were happy with

how he did it.

It's the weekend tomorrow so therapy drops off—but he'll have Monday, then the first doc apt on Tuesday, then another on Wednesday morning, then he'll have Thursday therapy and an all-important cardiologist appt on Friday. At least this week he won't have time to sit around and be bored.

They said he's due for his second covid shot maybe first week of Feb, which takes ONE load off my mind, I can tell you THAT much. I mean I know it isn't a magic bullet but hey. Under the circumstances that we're living, in I'll take 80-90% protection levels.

Me, I spent the day with my mom, dealing with her issues. She was going stir crazy so I said that if she kept her hands to herself and wore her mask religiously I would take her shopping (she is whining and WHINING how she "used to shop for herself"—well today was an object lesson as to why she no longer can. She doesn't know what she wants to buy, she literally asked me "is this a small cauliflower?...", she can't SEE the things on the shelves and what she sees she doesn't recognise as things she wants or needs. She was very subdued about the experience afterwards but honestly it was worth everything to take her out and prove to her that I am NOT confining her to her home out of some horrible instinct to torture her... and that this is no longer the world where you can just "pop out to the store" to get something you might need and have forgotten in the last trip. My grocery shopping forays are planned like military actions these days, I go in fast, get what I need, get OUT, and go only as often as I absolutely have to. But today... was a trial by fire. I don't know how long this will last and how long the memory will inform her attitude and stop her from whimpering at me and guilt tripping me about everything she can find a reason to guilt trip me for... honestly, a handful of hours with my mother, whom I really love a great deal, is enough to wipe me out for the next day.

Still. I got to run some of my own errands, I got to see my poor imprisoned darling and HE had a good day, and I'll take it as a win...

જી

24 January 2021

It's kind of drizzling snow outside, it's cold and wet and miserable, on my own again (never on a Sunday please)—and maybe I was inspired by Chaz Brenchley's odyssey I don't know but... I cleaned the fridge. There was at least one jar of Unidentified, lurking in the back, it didn't smell like anything familiar when I tried the sniff test, so out it went. I also found a cauliflower I have no memory of ever putting in there, and a bunch of what was once celery suffering from bad fridge burn (I tossed that out over the side of the deck. It's COLD outside. I know it isn't fit for human consumption but maybe some critter can make use of it...) I had a bad moment when one of the crisper drawers which came OUT all right showed no sign of wanting to go back IN again but I bullied it back onto its tracks. All good.

Now what am I going to do with the mushrooms I discovered lurking in there, and which have to be used, like, NOW, before they too begin to resemble something that only a wild creature in the woods might be tempted by...?

(just goes to show how absolutely DEMENTED the last little while has been. I've been eating haphazardly, and

the fridge was paying the price for it...)

❦

25 January 2021

Deck is back in hospital

❦

26 January 2021

..and everything crashed, and there's shatter on the floor and probably blood. I'm not sure where it came from. Possibly my hands when I tried to hold it all together.

They took Deck to the ER from the rehab place yesterday because his potassium levels were critically low (if it isn't one thing it's another. first his coag numbers were too high. Now his potassium is too low. He's taking a small pharmaceutical treasury of pills and somehow they simply cannot keep him in a stable state on these...) They tell me that often when they send people to the ER from that place they're gone for "a couple of hours" but if they wanted me to "hold his room" I had to pay premium (private pay) price for it. God knows I don't have the money to burn but I said ok hold it for one night (he was supposed to be back in a couple of hours, right?)

After five or six hours in the ER... they admit him to the cardiac ward again.

The doctor phoned me this morning. There's fluid on Deck's lungs. Possibly on the heart again.

It's heart failure.

They aren't allowing visitors to the hospital any more but they clear me for a visit because conversations need to be had. I go to see him today.

He's wretched and worn out, but he's still fighting. He still says he's going home. The doctor—once he finally arrives on the scene—basically tells him that going out of the hospital is going to be a revolving door from now on— nursing home/hospital/nursing home/hospital—because this is the new real. Going back to rehab doesn't seem to be much of a thing any more—they have simply basically said there isn't much point. Deck wants to come home. The doctor is skeptical of this. The only way he sanctions this... is on hospice.

Deck rebels at this because he doesn't want the one way street. Not yet.

It's his call. But I don't know where we go from here or how. I don't know if I can provide the care he needs by myself at home. I don't know how much hospice will provide or for how long. They're talking about possible caregivers—but PRIVATE ones that we'd have to pay for— and that is going to be pretty much out of reach.

I spent most of the day with him. When I left, it was with the understanding that I would probably not be allowed back in. This may be the last time I was able to hold his hand.

There is another procedure scheduled for tomorrow. He has to be off blood thinners (again) for this to happen. After that he's going to be in hospital for another day maybe two maybe three. After that...? I don't know. I really don't know. I am terrified, miserable, and I am basically just sitting here screaming "it isn't fair" at the universe.

I don't have the first clue what I am going to do with myself tomorrow.

I don't have the first clue how I am supposed to take care of him, if he does come home in three days.

I haven't the first clue how much time we have left but I have a horrible feeling we are looking at a very short tunnel here and the light at the end of it is an oncoming train.

I'm sorry. I am throwing all of this at you all. I don't know what else to do.

In theory I am supposed to go to bed soon and my head is splitting and my eyes are nearly swollen shut and I have lockjaw—my entire neck hurts from clenching my teeth so hard. I've been crying more or less the whole day. All I can say is that I held his hand. That may be all there is. That may be all that there will ever be, all that's left. I just have a godawful feeling I am waiting for THAT phone call now.

I told him I loved him. He told me he loved me.

There is nothing else that remains.

❧

January 28 2021

Okay.

Okay.

Not okay.

I was called in today for a palliative care consult at the hospital. Talked to a couple of people. I think we all agree that there is a slim-to-none chance that Deck would survive another full code, CPR, and that stuff. And so, scarily, his code was changed to DNR today.

They have pummelled his body. It is not responding the way they want. They are talking a reshuffle of meds. They took some fluid off his lungs and they took some scans today to make sure that there was no refluiding (like maybe bleeding) in lungs or heart and there isn't. That's the good news. Whether or not this will come back and how much they can or will do about that, we will have to see. The other good news is that the wound that sent him to the hospital in the first place seems to be more or less healed by now. At last. But, you know, that stopped being a priority of any sort a long time ago now. But I think that he has taken all that he can take, right now. He's bruised and black and blue everywhere, and he is just tired.

We are talking hospice care now, perhaps initially at hospice house as transition but then home. And then things start getting really interesting, I guess.

The house will have to be changed, for him. They are talking a hospital bed but that will be set up in his office— which means that some things need to be reshuffled. And for that, for all of that, for his comfort and his care... well, for those of you who want to consider that and are able to do so, I've put together a wish list on Amazon...

That which will help him the most is perhaps the gift of peace of mind, and for that to happen... a certain kind of financial backup for me needs to be in place... for after. Some complicated things are in play and essentially if he leaves me sooner rather than later—well—I can't get access to a survivor benefit of any sort until I turn sixty and that's still two years away. For those of you who are already there, he and I both thank you for that... but If I could get 80 more people to join my Patreon at $10/month tier... I'm going to be OK. (or more people, at $5. The arithmetic is flexible...) This would literally mean me keeping my house, *and my cats. Given the situation, my finding even a part time job at this point (unless it is editorial work done from home or something like that) is obviously not on the cards if I am also to be the caregiver here and that's a fulltime occupation by itself. Please, if you can, if you can even just do it for a period of a couple of years until I can access that other income... now is the time. For anyone who wants to see it, I have a listicle of where such income will go. And I promise I will keep up with new stuff on the Patreon, to make sure that you get value for your contribution. the link is at https://www.patreon.com/AlmaAlexander*

I took these photos today.

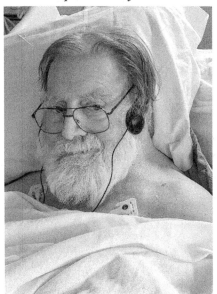

This was just before the palliative team came, and left. We were both much more somber, after. But you have to love the twinkle in his eyes here. That's still there. That's STILL THERE.

How long we can keep it there, I don't know.

I'll keep updating as I learn more. But now... is a practical moment. I need to get ready. For the undiscovered country.

Any help that anyone can give... we will take, at this point. With humility and gratitude.

I posted earlier that there was an owl right outside the window, calling out, calling out. I keep on thinking, now, if it was calling anyone's name.

I'm sorry if I sound dull and quenched at the moment. I'm a little overwhelmed. I'm numb, I know there are dozens of things to do right now, and I need to start doing them. But all I can think of—and it freezes me—is what

I am preparing FOR. And there are moments when I just stop breathing, at that thought.

It is entirely possible that this visit was the last one they will sanction at the hospital. I don't know what the timeframe for a discharge is. I may not see him for days, for a week, maybe. But it is entirely possible that when he does leave that hospital it will be for the last time - for procedures like this, anyway. And after that... what we have is what we have.

Hold us in the light, for as long as that is possible.

And if willing, if able, if you want to be part of the Deck army that brings him home to me and to what remains of his days on this earth—do whatever practical thing you might want to do. The list is there. At some point I will have to start trawling it and ticking stuff off. For now, it's there. Take a look if you are so inclined.

I love you all. I treasure you all. This has been a lifeline for me to an extent that you may not even understand. Thank you for that. And now I'm throwing it open to the universe.

ℭ♥

30 January 2021

So another update (Please, I feel very much like I'm inflicting these on the Universe by now. scroll on by if the word "update" is starting to make you twitch...)

I was in there again today and it was shocking, the change. Remember that twinkle-eyed picture I posted just the other day? I couldn't find that man. What greeted me was something much more hollowed out... and (a new thing) on oxygen. There was a mention—the first I heard—of something possibly concerning with his kidneys.

They've put him on morphine—why, I don't really know, because he says he isn't in pain as such. This is something I AM going to question. I am not a fan of overreach. The time may come when morphine is necessary and needed but I am not sure that time is now.

There are other meds questions I have. Two things appear on his meds list that sound very much like antibiotics—but I have heard no talk of infections anywhere as such so why is he on antibiotics? So far as I can tell they've taken him off blood thinners altogether. I have no clue why. But he is still on statins. which he doesn't like and doesn't trust, never has. So I have some questions, here.

I spoke to the hospice person. They may not have an opening for him in hospice house which may mean setting up at home next week and seeing what happens. But my love looked at me and for the first time in all of this mess said, "We may not have much time left". And it broke my heart into little pieces.

Ideally I would like him off morphine unless absolutely necessary (there have to be other ways of relieving even pain, unless it's REALLY bad, and just giving it for "comfort" is questionable, for me, because it is an appetite suppressant (and he isn't eating much anyway) and also because it can depress breathing ability and he already has enough trouble with that. And mostly because it's morphine, and it slows a mind up and pickles his spirit in dead brine. So long as he is not in pain and we still have time to share I would prefer it if he were himself and not adrift on a sea of laudanum.

I will be in to see him again tomorrow, and talking

with hospice again tomorrow, and trying to nail down something that needs to happen next week. If it's home then—and hey Bellingham people and Sudden Valley neighbors—I am going to need some help with moving a few items of furniture in order to accommodate a hospital bed. Is there anybody willing to help me do this? Additionally, is there anybody who needs an office chair? Possibly a small desk...?

I have made the acquaintance of a thoroughly amazing person who has already been above and beyond and is willing to continue to help me to care for Deck— especially if it turns out to be a shorter-term thing than anyone wants or expects it to be. But it's still going to be a bitter road. A lonely and bitter road.

That owl I mentioned the other day, he's back outside my window, calling constantly. I think I may be beginning to understand.

I said earlier that I found two lockers stuffed with packages when I went to get mail today. To all the people who were behind this part of the deluge, thank you. Thank you SO much. I can barely believe that you exist, that people like you exist. To whoever sent me the cookie tin— there was no name attached—thank you for the thought of that. I think I will be thanking people for the rest of his days. And the rest of mine.

I have absolutely no idea where I am going. I am holding a piece of paper on which only a part of the map is visible—the rest is a horrifying and terrifying void. I would like to think that maybe coming home will be an elixir, that he will pick up and come back. I don't want to put my hopes into that basket because I don't think I could bear it if they fell through the cracks of it. All I can do is wish, very, very hard. Alas, I seem to be all out of magic lamps and genies.

I am trying to hold onto the reality of him, of his presence, of his existence, of his love. But it's slipping away from me.

We always knew it might come to a pass, he is after all much older than I am and logically he was always going to "go first". But I am not ready for this now, if I ever could be ready for it at all. I am not ready. Not now. Not yet. everything in me aches; the heater is on in my office and directly aimed at me but my hands are cold, shock-cold, I can barely type this because my fingers are frozen into claws. I have no idea what will be waiting for me tomorrow.

30 January 2021, later

I will do an update later. But I just wanted to say...

I get my mail at a post box bank and they leave packages in package bins. Today I went to get mail and TWO PACKAGE BINS WERE STUFFED WITH THE WISHLIST STUFF.

I just stood there in front of the open locker brimming with packages and bawled.

ᏏᏠ

31 January 2021

Endgame part one.

I ran late this morning. There was an errand that needed doing in the morning and so I didn't turn up at the hospital until nearly half past 11, closer to 12.

Deck is breathing like a landed fish. Gasping. Gaunt.

Coherent, but it's increasingly difficult to make out what he's saying, and I have to ask him to repeat, several times. The nurse taking care of him tells me that he was largely non-responsive all morning, apart from one time when he asked the people taking care of him if he was being tortured, but that he "woke up" when I walked into the room.

It's raining outside. Miserably. HARD. The window is crying rivers of that rain on the glass.

Inside the room, I sit there and hold his hand, and bring cups of apple juice or ginger ale to his mouth when he gasps out the words of which he wants. I feed him some vanilla ice cream sitting there. But mostly I sit there beside him and look at him, and he looks back at me, and just whispers things to me.

"I love you"

"I promised you 25 years, love. I don't think that is happening. I think we... may have only hours..."

"I will love you forever."

Forever, this forever, the two of us here on this earth together, has lasted twenty years, six months, and eighteen days. They don't make forever like they used to any more.

The nurse comes back in and asks if there is anything that Deck needs.

"More time," he says.

The nurse says nothing, but above his mask you can read his eyes. I'm crying quietly. He grips my hand.

"I love you. So much."

You know the situation is dire when the hospital,

which has a firm policy of no visitors AT ALL, is now basically allowing me to come and go at will... and they have also bent the rules further still, in that they're allowing David in. His son. He's on his way. I texted him to tell him that I was there and did he want to talk to Deck on the cellphone (we've done that a few times) and he texts back that he's on his way, that he's going to be there about 1:30.

I try to cry off and give the two of them some time together, when David arrives at last. This is not mine alone—Deck may be my best friend and my love and the rock foundation of my world, but he is also a father, and this is a child losing a parent. Here, I've been before myself, and I know it is hard. But Deck is restless, twitchy; when I come back in, he calms, and David and I sit on either side of the bed, each holding a hand. Deck's gaunt face, his pouched exhausted eyes, turn from one to the other from us.

"I love you both so much," he says.

This room is saturated with love, and with grief.

He tries to keep us both in sight.

"So much... to say... so little," he says. Ungramatically. Perfectly understandably.

So much to say. So little.

"I love you."

David, who has a young son he is taking care of this week, then needs to go. Covid be damned, the two of us hug tightly in the anteroom where Deck can't see us, and hold onto each other for a long moment. We both know. We KNOW. It's written all over him.

I begged the people who had the power to make those decisions to take him into Hospice House, at least for a little while. I BEGGED them. It is a good place, my father died there seven and a half years ago and they were wonderful to him. It is a safe haven, a place where he can be cared for, kept comfortable, and maybe it IS just for a bridge, maybe he CAN beat this and come out the other side after all, and home will always be there, waiting. But he is on morphine now, and the endgame is starting to clarify, and going to a place where they understand endings and where he will have all the loving care that he needs may be the best possible solution under the circumstances. So at just past 3 pm that afternoon, they come for him, from Hospice House.

I tell them I'll meet them there, I have to swing past the house for some paperwork. I drive back to the house and it's still pouring with rain and inside the car I'm crying almost as hard. It's getting darker. The rain falls silver in the headlights. The world is grey, and fading.

I pick up the necessary paperwork, I give the bewildered cats some food, I grab Cupid (the little pink teddy bear he once gave me, the one who lives on our bed, the one who met a hard fate on our trip up the East Coast back when we were first married when Stan Kid's dog chewed off on of its poor eyes before we could rescue the poor thing. It matters to both of us, a meaningful little beast. So Cupid is coming with me.

And a couple of other things. More in the next post.

I head for Hospice House in the night and the rain.

Ⱳ

Endgame part two

When I reach Hospice House… in the rain… I am

met by the social worker and the nurse who has charge
of Deck. I am informed to be prepared, that during the
transport to Hospice House from the hospital (it isn't THAT
far, but it's far enough…) his oxygen sat levels dropped to
50 (if you don't know, normal for a human being is 96-
98—I spectacularly had 99 once—but they sent my father
straight to hospital when his was SEVENTY TWO and
Deck's had dropped twenty full points below that. This is
borderline oxygen deprivation. They brought him back up
to 80 when they got him there, but the damage… might
have been done already…

In the room, they've got him on an oxygen cannula
but he keeps on ripping it off and shaking his head that he
doesn't want it. I take his hand, and he squeezes it, but I
don't know if he is even aware of doing that. He keeps on
muttering, "I can't stand it, I can't stand it". They ask me
if I have funeral arrangements in place. I ask how long
they think he has. They tell me he's on morphine, and that
they can give him something else to bring his anxiety down
and help him rest. He clearly needs it, he's breathing with
audible little gasps of "aaah… ahhh…ah…" and quite
aside from it clearly being inadequate he is laboring to do
it. They tell me that it's quite possible that with a little rest
he will be breathing perhaps a little easier in the morning
but that the night to come… was anybody's guess. Choice:
stay or go? They have given him the anti-anxiety med. He's
lying in his bed under a handmade quilt, his head bowed,
his eyes closed, he looks like he's falling asleep. Cupid is
tucked at his shoulder, on guard.

The words tremble in the air, in the shadowed room.

So much to say… So little.

I love you.

I make the choice to leave, to try and grab some sleep, to come in early in the morning. But before I do that...

... this is for all of you who flocked to the Wish List. Honestly, those sheets must have been the only visible thing on the list for a while because I ended up... with FIVE OF THEM. So I took them to Hospice House and asked if they could use them for others who had a need, if those five packages of sheets could be used in lieu of a guerdon, the equivalent of two gold coins on Deck's eyes when he passes, his gift (and yours) to someone else whose clock may be running out of weeks or days or minutes. They took the sheets, and they took the package of bedsocks, and they promised that they will be put to use in Deck's name, in his memory. I hope you all don't mind. This was another of those celestial ransoms, this one for the easy passing of a great soul, and if it is measured in bedsheets and bedsocks, in the comfort given to other passages, then that is the unique and unusual price. Your names went forward into this handover, written as names of angels, and when all that was left was love... I gave love away. As bedsheets, perhaps. But make no mistake. My putting those up on a wishlist in order to make Deck's own existence comfortable... the way that wishlist was cleared within hours by people who wanted to make sure that this would happen... the way that Deck's own road was clearly unwinding... these things may have taken the shape of bedsheets but what I gave away was love.. Forgive me.

And so, I went home. In the dark, in the rain, crying.

I fed the cats again (they're comfort eating now). I cried. I eventually went to bed, and didn't sleep for a long time, just lying there staring out into the darkness of my room. At some point both cats crept in and curled up around me where they could find space, and purred quietly.

It was close to 1 AM that I think I finally drifted off...

... to be woken at 1:34 AM telling me that he was gone.

He was gone.

℘

Endgame part three

I did not sleep the rest of the night. I phoned David. And then I phoned some long-suffering friends who said I could call, whenever. When the phone rings at that hour, you don't need to be told, and when the person calling you is incoherently sobbing on the end of the line there's only one thing to know, and they knew. They held me in the shelter of their friendship for a moment, and then I went away again.

It was three am now. Four thirty. Six.

Deck had asked me to call a particular therapist he worked with at the rehab home and tell her thank you. I called the home and told THEM... and they all babbled what a lovely man he was and what a joy he was to care for which probably wasn't true because he was ornery and frustrated and unhappy there and "nice" might hot have entered into the equation, but they said it anyway. They said the therapist in question would be in at eight.

I phoned his insurance people, and got blessed with some deeply southern woman who heard that Deck had died and then just went into a long litany of "oh, lord. Oh, lord Jesus. Oh lord." while she was working on his account. When that was done I phoned the rehab place again, and got hold of the therapist, and gave her Deck's parting message. She sobbed on the phone, and I cried with her and

*we kind of whimpered at each other for a minute or two.
She said "he was SO special". I said I knew.*

*By this stage it was already close to half past eight,
and I got dressed and went out into (more) rain, or
maybe it was the same rain, maybe the universe hadn't
finished crying yet either. I stopped by the supermarket,
on my way, which had a florist—I wanted a yellow rose.
A single yellow rose. They had white, pink, red... but no
yellow. But this was important. So I made them take a
bouquet of yellow roses apart and give me one bloom. Let
me digress by telling you the story of the yellow rose. When
Deck and I first met face to face, in Vancouver, Canada,
when time came for us to part and me to go back to New
Zealand where I was living at the time and him to return
to Florida, I gave him a yellow rose as we said goodbye. For
me, it was a YELLOW ROSE and I gave him one because
I liked yellow roses. For him... he interpreted it in some
esoteric language of flowers, where yellow roses meant "I
like you but it's never going to be more than just friends".
He had put a lot of hopes and dreams into me already and
this threw him. He thought everything was over before it
had properly begun. It took a while to sort that mess out.
But in the end he knew what I knew—it was a yellow
rose, a yellow rose, a yellow rose, given with love because
the giver loved the flower and the person to whom it was
handed. And after that yellow roses belonged to both of
us. And now I was saying goodbye. And I wanted a yellow
rose, dammit all.*

*It was close to 9 o'clock when I finally came back to
Hospice House, and they took me through to his room.
They said he passed easily, asleep and then... beyond... and
I wept over his hand and kept repeating "I should have
stayed I should have stayed" and they said that there was no*

second guessing that. That nobody can know the hour. That it was okay. The chaplain person who was there said that she had been with centenarians when they died and those people who had lived that much longer didn't have half as much love as she could feel gathered in that room. She asked me to tell her about him, and I did, through sobs. I told her a funny story. She laughed. I brought in a slew of pages I'd taken off a funny calendar, day by day, and she went through them with me. And she said that we clearly shared a lot of laughter. And then she turned to him and said, "Deck, I'm not sure where you are right now, but this is evidence that every day you were not with your lady you were thought about, wished for, expected, held in faith. Few are given this. I understand now. I understand."

And then they left me alone with him, waiting for the funeral home people to arrive. Outside the window there was a suet birdfeeder, and at one point a woodpecker alighted on it, and I said to him, look, love, look, a woodpecker is on the feeder. Look, love, it's still raining. Look, love. Look.

When they came for him, they held the leaving ceremony they do at the hospice, where a body is wheeled out on its gurney on its last journey. They ring a bell three times to ring the passing of the soul. They asked me if I wanted to say anything. And I said, "I tell you I love you. I will not put that in the past tense because it will never be in the past. I will continue to love you. I always will."

And then I couldn't say anything else at all. And they took him. And he was gone. My yellow rose went with him, on the bier.

And I came out of the door, and stepped into a world without him.

And went home.

In the rain.

Loss

(The Hell of the

First Year After)

The Internet responded to the news. His friends from the long-lost Misc Writing circle weighed in:

Long ago, back in the very early '90s, when the internet was still pretty new to most people, I stumbled across a group of writer types chatting away on Usenet. I lurked for a while, and then tentatively sent a question to one of the regular, more vocal people there. And at that point, Deck became my very first cyberfriend. We never got to meet in person (though his wife, Alma Alexander, spent a week here with us during Minneapolis WorldCon), but had years of e-mail chats, and a few packages sent between Florida and Minnesota. I wonder how long he kept the little can of Spam that was an inside joke?

Deck left this world a bit after 1:30 Pacific time this morning. My heart breaks for dear Alma. And the world is a poorer place without this talented, intelligent, kind, funny man.

Godspeed, my friend.

LKB

~~~

Dammit.

Dammit.

Dammit.

The internet has been a boon, introducing me to far-flung friends across the globe.

And we just lost one of the very best of them. (Not Covid, however much that may matter.)

Watch over your girl, Deck.

AJB

❧

READING OVER THE WRITE-UP OF the process, in the previous section, it occurs to me that I was probably harsh in a lot of judgments—never let it be said that I was not grateful in every respect for any medical assistance that made Deck one ounce more comfortable or better off. But there were SO MANY comedies of errors in there. Like when he was taken off a blood thinner medication which he had been on—and had been stable on—for literally years and the medication was replaced by something new that I just happened to have noticed on TV ads and was a little taken aback at all the possible side effects even before I knew that Deck was being put on it—and when I queried that on several grounds (was there a generic equivalent? This was still a "going home" scenario and there was no way we could handle a really expensive non-generic big name drug, and they said they weren't sure, they didn't think so, they would look into it but if there wasn't an equivalent then he might have to be weaned off it and put back on his original medication when he was discharged which did beg the question why he would have been put on it in the first place and the ad I watched specifically warned against going off the drug on pain of even WORSE side effects—but I don't think we ever got a straight answer on that one, right until it became moot in any event). And all of that, ALL OF THAT, even without the final interference of the Covid era—and I

STILL maintain that despite the clear necessity of precautions the rules were applied capriciously and illogically when it came to the nursing home situation—if he was in full quarantine and no access was allowed then how come he was permitted to be taken OUT of that quarantine and taken in a van by a driver (these were early days, I am betting anything unvaxxed) to a doctor's surgery for an appointment where he interacted with a BUNCH of medical personnel who worked on him and also on a heap of other (non-quarantined) people and god alone knows who else in the waiting room, and somehow that contact was fine, but I, who was in direct contact with literally nobody that could possibly infect anything or anybody, was not allowed anywhere near him—don't they know I would have worn a HazMat suit or scuba gear to be permitted to go in and hold his hand if that was required…? Our last Christmas was stolen, our last New Year's Eve was smiles through a glass window, and I cannot forgive or forget that…

In the meantime, in the aftermath, blighted, blown apart, devastated, I continued to write updates.

❧

2 February 2021

> *I need to phone people. I need to cancel things (for instance, he doesn't need his cell phone any more). I need to do laundry and vacuum the house (it needs it badly). I need to do a thankfully short editing job that deadlines Feb 10 so I need to get stuck into that. I need to go clean out the cat boxes. I need to buy coffee (I thought I had more but I have maybe two more pots worth in the bag and since I am going through coffee like you wouldn't believe that's going to get me to maybe tomorrow. I need to go get my first covid shot tomorrow. I need to do computer housekeeping on things like my website (but oh dammit that was HIS*

job...)

I need to write about the last two days. I need to hold him close. I need to let him go.

I went to bed at half past one. I was up at six thirty. I watched the day creep into being from the maw of the night. Sleep is an idea, not an actual thing. And when I do sleep I start awake into a void.

I miss him. I miss him. I miss him. I miss him.

ↄ

8 February 2021

Day 7. Dear love you died a week ago or a hundred years have gone by, I am not entirely sure which. Too many minutes, too many hours, washed away in tears and now time is a landslide, and roads and rivers are buried underneath it, under a ton of mud and debris. Sometimes I think I recognise a piece of something sticking out of the mudflow. It's hard to be sure. Everything has changed, the landscape has changed utterly. The big trees that gave shelter are gone and the slope is bare and raw behind the gouge of the slide. Somewhere at the bottom of all that is a buried heart. Sometimes I can still hear it beating, very slowly.

Today, I gave away your office chair to somebody who knew you, who said it would be special because it used to be yours. Today, I am watching the temperature gauge slide and worrying about the pipes—yes, you would have told me to leave the tap dripping. I will. But you were the one who always said everything would be okay and I was always the one who fretted. Nobody's telling me it's going to be okay any more. Today, I went into the living room

and picked up all the books that you had waiting for you
there, that you were going to read when you "got better
glasses". I put them back on the shelf. The glasses don't
matter any more. Yours, the ones that came home with
me from the hospice, are watching me from your desk. It's
hard to endure their gaze. Today, the temperature fell below
freezing and I still had that large bottle of apple cider I
had bought in order to make mulled cider when you came
home. You aren't coming home for mulled cider ever again.
So I made it tonight, for me, and sat there sipping the
warm spicy thing and seasoning it with tears.

Today, it's been a week.

It's been a hundred years.

❧

16 February 2021

Dear love, you seem to have gone missing so long ago
and yet it's just over two weeks ago that you left me. And
today... is hard. wicked hard.

Happy birthday.

I had a card. I always had a card. This one is resting
propped up against the urn containing your ashes, maybe
hoping it'll get through to you by osmosis or something—
except I'm not sure that the grief is a wall standing in
its way right now. I'm telling you happy birthday and I
am not sure if you are listening, if you can hear, if some
part of you still lingers here and sees that silly card that I
hoarded—I have one for the next birthday, too. For the
re-birthday coming up in June. For the 21st anniversary
that would have happened in July. They live in my bedside
cabinet drawer—when I found good cards I bought them

*and then hoarded them against the occasions that would
come up, that we'd share. There is a box of cards of the
past sitting in your closet—I dare not touch it right now. I
might add this last unseen card—this LAST card—to that
pile at some point. I have no idea right now. I'm trying to
get through the day one minute at a time.*

*I just read an article on Star Trek - not YOURS
(TNG) or MINE (the original series) but one we both
loved, Deep Space 9—and once again the instinct was
to hit the share button, to email it to you—and I really
have to go and clean out your inbox now it has to be
drowning—but the problem is that yours was the address
for a bunch of official stuff and I am not sure how to
change it if I can at all without losing an account I need—
ah, love, you left a bit of a mess here...*

*Happy birthday. I know it's only the first of many
without you. But it's the first. And it may be the hardest.*

༄

19 February 2021

*So I sailed out to do a couple of errands today... and
I saw that the chocolate shop downtown was open. They
have these massively wonderful little bite-sized hazelnut-
creme-filled dark chocolate hedgehogs which I am an abject
worshipper of, so I go inside to check out if they had any.
They did. They also had hazelnut dark chocolate "bark"
which is also amazing so I got a pack of that. So the guy
behind the counter says, you like hazelnut? We JUST
made this hazelnut chocolate gelato—how about it? And
then I noticed something called "sipping chocolate" on
their chalk-written in-store 'menu' and asked what that
was and he said, "liquid ganache". The place was empty*

*except for me and I asked if I could have it there—and
he said yeah, they were allowed indoor seating now with
proper distancing but at any rate there was nobody else
there to distance FROM so I sat there at the counter by the
window, eating gelato, sipping this evil ganache concoction
that I really could probably live on if I had to and wouldn't
call it hardship—looking out onto the street, at people
(very few people) passing by, just like it was the good old
days. Except... for the fact... that two of those people looked
scruffy and dirty, and they paused to look into the trash
can outside the window of the chocolate place with an air
of hoping that they might... find something... useful in
there. One of them was even wearing a mask—one of those
single-use throwaway blue paper ones but this one looked
like it had been worn well past its sell-by date. At least he
was making an effort, of sorts, although I am not at all
certain how effective it might have been.*

*I needed that, the idea that I could sit down and
have a cup of drinking chocolate in a coffee shop. But it
still feels like I stepped into a different world through a
mirror. Things might look the same, but NOTHING is the
same. Nothing is ever going to be the same again. Partly
it's because *I* am different, but partly it's the world itself,
twisted and wrung by this disease, by all the things that
came clinging to its coat tails.*

*I felt a little like a jigsaw piece from an entirely
different puzzle, trying to fit myself into a picture where I
no longer belonged. The guy who served me at the counter
wore a wedding ring. I did too but I stared at mine and
realised that it was no longer "true". It was a dowager
wedding ring, no longer a regnant one.*

*Everything is different. And older. and greyer. and
more worn. And less true. And sadder. And lonelier. and*

more dangerous. And more wicked.

It is a world that still has hazelnut chocolate hedgehogs and sipping chocolate. But was that little aftertaste there before? Did I not notice it because of the overlay of the good and the sweet... or is it a new thing, now? Is this what loss tastes like? Is everything going to taste of loss from this moment on?...

❧

9 March 2021

Did anyone here watch "The Durrells of Corfu"? It was a joy. Of course, it was based on Gerald Durrell's writings—which I had read, but which Deck had not, and he had no real idea about the Durrell family before this series, and had never connected Lawrence Durrell and Gerald Durrell (both of whom he had HEARD of) as being part of the same family. I'd read the books but a LONG time ago and I'd forgotten most of it and the idiosyncrasies of Corfu coming to life onscreen were an ongoing delight. But if you watched it to the end, you will recall the scene on the beach, the one where Louisa Durrell and Spiros made their farewells to one another—deeply connected, kept apart by circumstances and context and finally having spoken out of their love for one another and then the hammer of the war descends and Louisa has to leave... and Spiros has to stay.

That goodbye. That goodbye on the deserted beach. It ripped your heart out.

But then Spiros said something, tenderly, lovingly, inexorably. It was hard to part... but... "Would you rather we had never met?"

I dreamed of that scene last night.

I know, Deck. I know what you're telling me.

And you know the answer to that question. But don't expect me to give it willingly. Not now. Not yet.

☙

13 March 2021

You know what's utterly barmy? I drove to Mom's today (to fix her clocks for the stupid time change tonight (and now she is REALLY lost and doesn't know WHAT time it is or what day of the week—I mean, yeah, thanks for THAT, *all* I needed right now…) and my road from here to there takes me past an intersection on one side of which is a parking lot that ties together various unrelated things like a hotel, an Olive Garden restaurant (honestly people if you want people to read a sign you put up basically don't make it white print on pale green background—In direct sunlight it's just one pale smear…), the ex-offices of the AAA (they have kinda gone full digital, the premises look rather empty and forlorn right now)… and the Wound Clinic.

The Wound Clinic, where the entire leg wound odyssey began five years ago, where the spiral returned us in the last few months of last year, where I'd go to sit in the waiting room when they took Deck in for his appointments in the hope of snatching a moment with him while he waited for his transport back to the nursing home lockup (hey, if other unrelated people could be in the waiting room… so could I…)

And there I am sitting at the red light next to the entrance to this parking lot, clutching the steering wheel with both hands, my jaw clenched tight, and my cheeks streaked with tears I didn't even realise had spilled.

This town, these streets, my life, are filled with the shadows he left behind.

❧

21 March 2021 (my blog)

The Dichotomy of Grief

For those who come here regularly, you might have noticed that the blog has been a little sparse lately. That's because I lost my partner, my love, my husband... my webmaster... the man who was in literal charge of this site on a day to day to week to month to year basis, who would pull me up with "I need a blog post for Sunday" every week, who did the heavy lifting, who... who... who was everything.

He's gone, and I've spent the last four month since he went into the hospital maw, and the last TWO months since he left me for good, in a tight knot of grief and pain and misery and loss. I'm sorry I haven't kept up with the website the way I should. At first I was too busy racing here there and everywhere trying to keep up with his medical and administrative needs, and then afterwards... this was his place, his space, and it HURT to tinker with it...

I haven't written poetry in a long time. I tend to write poetry when I NEED to, when the feelings run too high for anything else to do when it comes to communication.

I wrote a poem today.

I thought I'd share it with you.

The Dichotomy of Grief

I don't want to remember.
I want to shut down memory
All the bright sparks of precious moments
That come to haunt me unexpectedly
When I least expect it
When my defenses are down
When everything that comes flooding back is a stab
A sharp pain like an icicle to the heart
Every word, every quick glimpse of a smile,
Every glance, every shared moment,
Every lilt of laughter,
It hurts too much
To know it is gone for good
It hurts too much
I don't want to remember
Anything.

I want to remember
I want memory to be eternal
Every single thing we both loved
Every single thing we both knew
Every instant of your caring, and your sincerity, and your
pride
Every memory watching snow fall
Or listening to birds singing in the summer trees
Every cup of mulled cider on a winter twilight
Every plate-sized golden autumn leaf I brought inside
From where it was shed from our big maple
It heals me
To know that these things existed
It heals me
I want to remember
Everything.

He used to say something, often, to the point where he was KNOWN for it.

So I made a picture.

Nothing bad ever
happens to a writer.

It's all material.

Deck Deckert

I miss him. So much.

Ꮽ

24 March 2021

It's 10 PM, I've just got the final versions of the covers for the reissue of the Worldweavers series, the Fairy Tale book is so NEARLY here, the Changer of Days rights are finally with me and I can start planning that 20th anniversary edition of that... and dear GOD, Deck, I miss you. I hate it that you won't be here for any of this. I purely HATE it. I hate the hole you left in the universe. I pour the joy into it and it sucks it up now and every last atom of it vanishes into the void instead of getting reflected back at me, as it should be, as it always was. I'm sorry, but for twenty years I had that. It's hard to adjust to the sheer absence of you.

❧

13 April 2021

Closed down an online account today with Deck's name on it.

The death of a thousand deletions.

❧

16 April 2021

Dear love

You'd keep a hand on my knee when we travelled in the car. I'd curl up at your feet leaning on your leg when we watched TV. Half-asleep, we'd reach out for each other's hand at night. I'd hug you randomly from behind as you sat in your armchair. You'd wrap your stroke impaired right arm at the wrist with the fingers of your good left hand and hold your arms around me even when you could not make the right arm obey your command to do it by itself.

In your hospital bed I'd fight my way past enveloping blankets and pillows and twisting IV lines to hold your poor bruised hand. During the time that they wouldn't let me near you in the rehab place I'd lie in bed at night and 'hold' your hand between mine, leaving the space where your hand would have been, a ghostly presence there in the dark, hoping you could feel my fingers curling around yours.

In hospice, I held your hand, cold and marble white, in silence while I waited for you to leave on your final journey.

If either of us reached out, the other was there. We touched. All the time. Right until the end.

I miss the presence of you.

ℭℕ

5 May 2021

So, then.

I just fell down the stairs.

Before anyone freaks out, I'm fine. My ankle hurts a bit but I have full range of motion, I bent my finger a bit, and I spilled some coffee but did not smash the coffee cup. I'm fine, it's all fine. But I fell down the stairs, and I sat there for a moment considering things.

It's all fine. And it isn't as though Deck could have done much, as and of himself, to help if things had NOT been fine at any point—but he could have called 911 if necessary, he could have opened the door to any paramedics that might have arrived in response, he could have dealt with the problem of the cats (as in their not escaping out the front door while it was hanging open to admit said paramedics, all of that. But *I don't have that backup anymore*. If I needed to call anyone I would have had to drag myself to a phone, somewhere. I would have had to deal with the problems of ingress of any potential help (and remember, I just put dowels in all the windows—nobody can just crawl into this house any more...)

My life is different. I no longer have anyone near, to help. I do it or it doesn't get done. And if I break a limb in this house or do other damage... things just escalated from disastrous to potentially catastrophic.

I'm fine. REALLY. I'm here typing, no? you can tell I'm not in pieces or in agony. But I did just fall down the stairs.

So there's that.

ↁↃ

10 May 2021

I was futzing around my email inboxes. They are mostly overfull and need cleaning out—all except one, the one named "Deck", where a lot of old messages still reside and now are more treasured than ever.

I'm going to share Deck with you. Here's a message from May of 2001... back in Florida...

ↁↃ

"It started when a couple of guys from Adelphia Cable...

No, that wasn't the start of it. It began when my ISP decided to dump me...

No, it started before that when I tried to install a new hard drive...

Unh, no, actually it started earlier than that when we tried to network our two computers...

Well, whatever, whenever... for the first time in more than three weeks, I have both a functioning computer, an Internet connection, and email.

I think I told you about that networking attempt. If I didn't, thank your lucky stars. It was a disaster and Alma's computer and mine are not yet intimately connected. And it cost me a few days without a computer.

We pulled the offending, and apparently offended, ethernet board and my computer went cheerfully back to work.

Except...

While trying to solve the network problem, I was told, erroneously, that I needed to upgrade to Windows 98 and I reluctantly did so. "No more room on Drive C," Windows began screaming at me when I tried to do the simplest thing.

"But I've got a two-gig hard drive," I screamed back. "How the hell did you fill that up?"

There was no answer—Windows doesn't deign to listen to mere users. So I bought a 20-gig hard drive and tried to install it. You've heard that part of the tale. Windows thought the hard drive was a floppy and it stopped talking to the real floppy. While trying to straighten that out, I jiggled something or another and then nothing worked.

Thank god my son, my original computer guru, came down from Seattle for a visit. "You've moved the atmafras out of the combobulator and that messed up the juwkienwatz," he said, pushing his pointed wizard hat back on his head. "But," he added, "I don't know what the hell you did to the power supply."

He muttered and poked and prodded, said magical incantations, and typed mysterious symbols from an ancient forbidden language—and my computer was resurrected. You can read more about that at http://bookofresurrection.homestead.com/ RESURRECTION.html *[[AA FOOTNOTE: *I* wrote that up. of course the link no longer exists...]]*

Then my ISP decided to dump me. One day I had email, the next day I didn't. Cybergate had told us customers earlier that they were going out of the dialup business and had sold us all to a new plantation, Earthlink. Our new owners would be contacting us shortly to lay out the terms of our servitude, they said blithely. But no Word from on high reached my email in-box and I assumed there had been some delay at the auction house. Then, poof, no email.

I was able, however, to dial in to my late and unlamented server and surf the web, and to receive email via an account at another server. Don't ask, I don't know. I just could.

Receive, but not send!

Not to worry, I told Alma. I'll just get a high-

*speed cable connection and get back in contact
with the world. Hah! Again I refer you to http://
bookofresurrection.homestead.com/RESURRECTION.html*

*While sitting at my computer one morning, still
making some kind of a magical connection to the
World Wide Web through a non-existent ISP, I turned
to Alma and started demonstrating my technique as a
high school viola player—sans a viola. "I always had
to play the second fiddle parts," I said. "The violins
soared and sang, and I played an endless variation
of 'ta ta, ta ta, ta ta.'" I demonstrated, holding out
my left arm to cradle the invisible viola, swinging my
right, bow, hand with impeccable technique.*

*Alma began poking me. Rude of her, I thought.
And then a voice behind me at the open office
door said: "Cable man. Now that you've got the
bougainvillea cut back, I'll just get on with it, shall
I?"*

*I should have seen the expression on his face,
Alma said, chortling. That was nearly 72 hours ago
and she is STILL chuckling!*

*The bougainvillea bush was cut back only on one
side, however, and the cable man was forced to thread
his cable through brambles and thorns that have been
known to puncture truck tires. Bleeding and torn he
came back to announce the job completed. He didn't
mention my concert.*

*I was reconnected to the web. I could surf the
web at a faster rate (but not faster than a speeding
bullet as I had been led to believe) and I could even
send email.*

Send, but not receive!

*I spent an hour waiting for a techie at Adelphia
support to talk to me. And then I spent a half hour
inserting all the new settings in Agent and Eudora
that I needed for newsgroups and email.*

The net result?

I could send, but not receive!

*And my computer was repeatedly crashing as
a confused Windows decided it was terminally ill,
turned blue and shut down.*

*"I'll call them for you," my beloved bride said
soothingly, apparently alarmed that I was screaming
nearly incoherently, except for the anatomically
impossible suggestions I was making to Bill Gates.*

*She called back the cable people and two hours
later, a miracle:*
I could send
and I could receive email!
You're probably not as happy as I am, of course.
But it's good to talk to you again.
Deck

☙

17 May 2021

*…for a moment there, searching for a password on
Deck's computer, I thought I'd accidentally deleted the very
thing I was looking for which would make life just that
little more difficult. There was a time I could have done
this sort of thing in my sleep. I'm just losing brain cells
every day, it feels like, especially when it comes to doing
things to clean up what remains after Deck has left the
building. I keep on getting… distracted… by fugue states…
wondering what in holy hell am I doing digging around
in his computer… why am I here… why is he not… why
can't he do what's nec… oh. right. And then I remember.
And when I "Wake" up from this I get faced with the
ohmigodIdeletedthethingIneeded scenario without ever
being completely aware that I was anywhere near doing
it…*

☙

16 June 2021 (my blog)

It's literally been years…

..since I've written much poetry. Writing poetry is something I tend to do in the grip of strong emotion—and god knows I'm there now—but my skills are rusty at best.

Here's a raw draft I produced of one, trying to grasp the parameters of that raw kind of grief which doesn't seem to be diminishing or shifting, just stalled in place like a malevolent storm that's stuck RIGHT overhead as a Cat 5 Hurricane and is still blowing debris about even after it's already destroyed everything on ground zero below.

In time, maybe, I will regain the ability that I had where I could lay hold of words and make them dance to a tune I dictated to them. But right now—in the throes of that unhealed grief—I'm barely able to touch them, let alone arrange them, or make them do anything they don't want to do. So you'll have to forgive poetry for trying to measure up to that—but writing poetry is possibly the only thing that a wounded writer's soul can bring to bear, the only weapon I have left to me.

So—if you've ever lost someone you loved—family, or friend, or pet—or even lost a life you treasured and had to rebuild it from scratch all over again—I call you my people. I'm sorry this isn't polished but it may never be— that isn't what it is for. Perfection isn't a measure for the poetry of grief.

I LIVE IN A PLACE WHERE TIME

I live in a place where time has gone feral—moments crawl by
In what feels like months, or years;
And centuries pass malevolently in the time it takes

For an eye to blink back tears.
I remember clearly things from long ago, while memories
Of yesterday are a blur of pain—
I ache for the kind of hours, the kind of days,
Which will not come this way again.
A life is built of instants, one by one, a smile, a word, a glance–

Memories, hopes, and dreams–

They become, in time, a woman, or a man
Who are so much more than they seem…
a lifetime
In the shape of a single day,
Who shares eternities, which fly too fast, and then too slow
When they leave you and go away.

I live in a place where time has frozen and I wait
In the still center of whirling centuries
Waiting for the day to fade, and the seasons to turn,
Dying leaves falling from bare trees.
The road I walk is empty, and frightening, and dark
Without your light to guide me–
I live in a place where time has stopped
Without you beside me.

വ

    20 Jun 2021

    So, I ran away from home today Sorry, baby cats.
You were on your own today. The silence and emptiness
was too much, on this day, on the day when it would have
been Deck's 18th re-birthday as we called it, eighteen years
since the stroke happened. I got him a card for it every

year, and it was easy in the beginning (there are "special"
cards for the very young—so he got a "first" birthday, a
"second", a "third"... a "fifth"... a "seventh".. a "tenth"... a
"thirteenth"... a "fourteenth", a "fifteenth", a "sixteenth"...
the years in between were not specifically easy to find and
I had to improvise. But there WERE special 18th birthday
cards. Of course there were. And I had one ready for today.
I HAD THE CARD. I would usually leave these cards
propped up against his computer the night before so that
he would find them when he woke up in the morning (he
always woke up at ungodly hours of the morning...) and
then he would wait to open them until he brought my
coffee in in the mornings when I woke up as he always did.

This time... I didn't leave a card out. There was
nobody to open it. Nobody to smile over it. Nobody to
chuckle with over it in the morning over coffee.

I had two hours sleep last night. I could not close my
eyes. I could not bear the absence.

This morning I fled. I just picked up my phone and
my bag and my keys and I fled, into the woods, out to the
seashore, anywhere, anywhere except here where he was not
and there was no card to open this morning.

And then, as I sat down to eat some ice cream in
Fairhaven to try and satiate the hunger that could not be
satiated... there's these two Christianist idiots standing on
the street corner, waving bibles and blathering about "god's
plans". I swear it took every ounce of self-control not to go
over there and take that stupid book and start hitting them
upside the head with it. I have little patience with that
anyway—you are always free to believe whatever you want
but your freedom to push your faith stops when you start
invading MINE and trying to stuff your "truth" down my

gullet. But today of all days... I am sitting there numb with emptiness and someone wants me to think this was god's "plan"? Sorry. I have no interest in that god.

It was close. I nearly, nearly lost it with them. In the end I just turned away and fussed a dog who had come out of surgery and had an idiotically shaved leg and seemed so very self-conscious about it. I turned my back on the happy clappies and if only my ignoring could have had a WEIGHT on it. It would have crushed them.

How dare you tell me that, now. How DARE you. How dare you sanctimoniously sit in judgment of my loss and my hurt. HOW DARE YOU.

I don't pray, as such, not formally, but here's a prayer—may God reach out to you and make you understand what you were doing today. May he make you feel that pain. May he make you feel every morsel of it, and then magnify it tenfold. may he make you understand that you were not put here to pontificate about God to people who do not wish to hear your empty dogma (oh, and by the way—thank you for the laugh that was embedded in there. "The bible is filled with scientific facts"?... REALLY???)

Anyway. I'm exhausted. I'm hurting. But I suspect that I am in for another sleepless night...

ℰℐ

3 July 2021

...so far I've cleaned litterboxes at 4 AM, watched infomercials for ugly jewellery I would NEVER wear because I couldn't sleep and this was somebody talking in the silence, made cups of coffee and left them on the counter while I wandered off to do... something else... and coming

*back to find a stone cold full cup of coffee hours later,
driven aimlessly in a random direction until I start crying
too hard to drive and then find a place to stop and sob it
out, looked at the last stash of wine bottles in our wine
rack which would ordinarily have taken the two of us six
months or more to get through and wondering what to DO
with them (what, I'm supposed to drink them all alone?),
gone to sleep in tears, woken up in tears, handed over his
flannel shirts to someone to have a quilt made from them
and then wept as they went out the door... insane? I am
probably certifiable.*

[A response to that entry from a friend:

*Alma Alexander: Completely understandable, and
forgiven. When my dad died, an MD friend gave me
a handout about grief from the American Academy of
Family Physicians. It included the factoid that there's some
culture—I don't remember which—where bereaved people
are considered legally insane for a year after the death, not
because they're considered mentally ill, but because that
gives them permission to behave in ways that wouldn't be
tolerated otherwise: storming out of meetings, calling people
at 3 a.m. to sob, forgetting where they left everything, etc. I
wish our own culture were as understanding of grief.—SP]*

ↇↄ

*Book View Café blog, 7 July 2021: "sky burial on July
14"*

*In every relationship there are stories of what "came
before", the things that defined the person you are currently
in a relationship with, before you met them. Sometimes
you'll hear these stories second hand. Sometimes the person
in question will tell you the stories that meant the most.*

My husband did skydiving when he was young. It all started when he (then a young journalist) got given/ got cajoled into/picked up a story about skydiving—and thought he wanted to try it out for himself before he wrote the story. The flirtation turned into a full-fledged love affair, and he went on to make many jumps. His stories about that part of his life included:

the time he landed on a watermelon. SQUARELY. It shattered, of course, and he wore Watermelon Bottom all the way as he trudged back to base, after—followed by a squadron of curious bees who were taking rather too close an interest in his butt.

…the time he landed on the "wrong" side of a canal bisecting a field—the base camp was across the canal and maybe a ten-minute walk across the field. Alas, the canal was deep, so it could not be waded but had to be swum, and just wide enough that it couldn't be leaped over, it had to be swum. This was a problem in that the water that had to be swum in… contained water moccasins. Hubs elected to walk the long way around, rather than chance the encounter with a snake which took exception to his invasion of its habitat.

…the time he and his friend went up to do a jump that would prove just how "safe" skydiving was, to the parents of an 18-year-old girl who wanted to try it. Unfortunately, his pal saw, as he was coming in to land, that he was about to land squarely on a cow skull complete (somehow) with horns—either way, not a good place to hit the ground. He twisted sideways to avoid it, and landed on the wrong ankle, badly, so came limping back to the aforementioned parents with assurances that he was absolutely fine but grimacing with the pain. Hubs had issues with his main parachute, and then realised that his

emergency chute cord had tangled itself around his leg—but he had no choice but to pull that, and as a consequence garrotted his knee with it, so HE came limping back to base assuring the parents that yeah this was REALLY safe. I can't say I would have believed those two wrecks, if I had been that girl's parents.

…the time he landed on the tarmac, with his hip and thigh leading—when he showed the purple hip-to-knee bruise to his friend, afterwards, the friend CALLED HIS WIFE and made hubs drop trou to reveal the spectacular size and colour of it to the woman.

There's more. He had a lifetime of these stories. And he loved every moment of it, he would tell me in great sensual detail what it felt like to fly through the bright air before the chute kicked in, the sounds, the sight, the touch of the sky as he fell through it down towards the waiting earth.

This was also the man who owned his own plane for a little while.

This was a man who, before his eyes stopped cooperating fully much to his regret and he could no longer see them clearly, would spend long silences gazing raptly up into the night sky full of stars. This was the man who went to several launches at Cape Canaveral, including a night launch, and told me all about that, too.

He was always in love with wings, with flight, with the sky.

Burying him in the ground would have been a crime.

So I contacted a local skydiving club and asked if they would be willing for somebody to scatter his ashes on a jump. One last skydive, for the man whose soul lived up there, the man who'd always had wings—at the very least, I felt them closing around me, when we got married, protecting and cherishing me, guarding me from the winds of the world. They were there right until he died. The memory of them is there still, will always be. And the last thing I could do for him was... this. Giving him back to the sky that he loved. So that every time I took a breath of air or looked up at the moon or caught the smell of frost in autumn mornings or felt the touch of wind brush past my cheek... he would be there. He would always be there. He is gone from my side, but he will now be all around me.

Good bye, my love, and may the stars shine the brighter for the presence of your bright soul which will fly amongst them.

❧

And then, of course, I wrote up the occasion itself:

14 July 2021 (My blog)

The Last Moment

14 July 2021 Deck's last jump:

I am a creature who lives stretched across time. I can remember vividly things that took place decades ago—down to conversations, the tone of voice in which they were had, the sound of remembered laughter. I am forever projecting into the future—my "panic now it saves time later" mantra has been the subject of much gentle mockery by all too many people who know me. The one thing I never mastered properly was arguably the most difficult one of all, the grasping of a single moment of existence and living in it fully and completely, in a way that makes that moment all that there is, was, ever will be. The most important sliver of time that could exist, the one that

*surrounds you RIGHT NOW, that matters RIGHT NOW,
that is here now and never was here before or will be (or
could be) ever again.*

*My beloved used to smile at me and say, "I know why
I was put on this earth. It's to teach you how to treasure the
moment." Because he was someone who could. He could
hold time like a raindrop in his hand, rapt in its beauty,
watching it sparkle and glow in the light, appreciate the act
of its existence and of his act of sharing in that existence.*

*He never did succeed in the task that he claimed he
was put here to accomplish. I never really learned that
untrammeled joy of being, unburdened by regrets (because
if you lived the moment right you could not have any to
haunt you) or any kind of dread (because if you lived the
moment right, there was nothing coming down the pike
that could hurt you). That was him, that was his light, that
was the light in which I happily curled, safe and protected
in its bubble. He didn't teach me how to do it—I don't
think it's teachable. But its protection was wrapped around
me like angel's wings for twenty years, and for twenty years
he held the moment, and kept me there beside him, holding
on.*

*Right until it cracked wide open. And the raindrop
shivered and found the crack and melted through it and
was gone.*

*We had not spoken much about the "Aftermath"
of things, as it were—but there was a conversation or
two. The "what do you want me to do with you, after"
conversation. And he said he didn't much care, really; and
I said, I am going to find somebody to throw you into the
sky. And he said, that would be nice. It wasn't so much of
a firm promise, but it was a sort of silent vow. I was not*

going to put this bright spirit into the ground, because he was of the air, you see.

Deck did his first skydive more than half a century ago, as a reporter for the Palm Beach Times who got told about this jumping-out-of-a-perfectly-good-airplane thing by a neighbor of his, and saw only the potential of a story for his paper—but initially that was all it was, a story, and, as he put it, "It would make a good photo feature for my paper. I certainly had no intention of pulling such an idiotic stunt myself."

He carries on to say, in the story that he did write for his paper (I have the original, a TYPED original, this was way before computers and word processing…), in his own words:

"*My sense of high adventure is to go out in the rain without an umbrella. And, as a colleague unkindly but accurately pointed out, among the New Frontiersmen I more accurately resemble Pierre Salinger than Bobby Kennedy.*

But, in attempting to gather material for a story I continually ran into a stumbling block… Every time I asked a skydiver why he did it, a dreamy look would come into his eyes, he'd mumble incoherently for a moment and then sigh helplessly, 'You can't explain it. You'll just have to try it yourself.'

After hearing this several times I finally decided—with all the enthusiasm of a soldier volunteering for a suicide mission—that that was exactly what I was going to have to do.

I began training after convincing Brad Marshall, president of the local club, that my reason for jumping was a legitimate one. He had his doubts about a reporter jumping just to write a story, not realizing that for a reporter the best reason in the world for doing anything is to get a story out of it.

It was when we got to emergency procedures that I had second thoughts about what I was about to do. Talk about what to do if your main chute doesn't open, or if you are landing in water, a tree, or a power line is nothing likely to encourage a novice jumper.

Marshall, who has had plenty of experience in training new jumpers (he once aided in training one of the stunt jumpers on the TV show Ripcord), helped me out with my equipment the day of the jump.

Another student static line jumper and the jumpmaster of the flight, Nelson Parrish, and I crammed our way into the small four-passenger plane and were taken up to 2400 feet where a wind streamer was released.

At 2800 feet the other student jumped out and I completed the intricate maneuver of changing places within the confined quarters, an operation so difficult that I had vague hopes of having my jump cancelled because I couldn't get into position.

Up until that point I believed myself quite calm. Perhaps I was. But if so, it's strange that I remember so little about getting out of the plane.

When the command came to go I remember moving my feet cautiously out of the door of the plane and feeling them whipped back by the wind. I reached for the strut of the plane to pull myself out and the next thing I knew I was falling. The jumpmaster swears he didn't push, and the pilot contends he didn't roll the plane. I have a horrible suspicion that I didn't jump but simply fell.

I had received careful instruction on how to fall so as to remain stable, face to ground. To no avail. I felt myself turning over on my side and flailed my arms helplessly.

It was at that point that I felt the light tug and then the heavy jar as the static line did its job of pulling open my chute. I just hung there for a moment in stunned disbelief that it had all actually happened.

I looked up at the chute seemingly miles above my head and it was the most beautiful sight I'd ever seen in my life... except the sides kept on folding in and out. That scared me so much I never looked up again.

I finally remembered to look for the DZ (drop zone) and its white target and found it a half mile or so southwest of me— and a thousand miles straight down. I reached cautiously up the risers and found the control line that allowed me some steerability and headed towards the target. I was amazed at how easily they moved the chute, and I began oscillating as I turned too fast. For a moment I was afraid I was going to get seasick.

The rest of the ride down was uneventful... except I was off target, it happened too fast, and I landed in a heavy patch of palmettos. After landing surprisingly gently I picked myself up and just stood there in something of a daze until Marshall found me.

Though a first jump is like no other and static line parachuting cannot be compared to the free fall of real skydiving, I found a little of what keeps a sky diver coming back.

When the chute first opens you hang suspended in a world that is completely insulated from the humdrum of ordinary existence. The world below has a virginal beauty that disappears upon closer examination. But it is the silence that grips you, a silence so perfect, so rare and so ethereal that you hug it to yourself in a futile attempt to keep it forever.

For a brief moment you enter a world whose existence only the poets before you had discovered and which only the poets can describe.

I only wanted a story. But if it's a nice weekend I'm going to make my second jump.

Why?

Well, like we said... you just can't explain it. You'll just have to try it yourself."

jump (5)

Though a first jump is like no other and static line parachuting
can not be compared to the free fall of sky diving, I found a little
of what keeps a sky diver coming back.

When the chute first opens you hang suspended in a world that
is completely insulated from the humdrum of ordinary existence. The
world below has beauty that disappears upon closer examination. But
it is the silence that grips you, a silence so perfect, so rare and
so ethereal that you hug it to yourself in a futile attempt to keep
it forever.

For a brief moment you enter a world whose existence only the
poets before you had discovered and which only the poets can describe.

I only wanted a story. But if its a nice weekend I'm going to
make my second jump.

Why?

Well, like we said...you just can't explain it. You'll just
have to try it yourself.

###

That… was a beginning. A beginning of a love affair with the sky, with flight, that lasted his whole life. He went on to make many jumps, after, and told me story after story about it.

He had a lifetime of these stories. And he loved every moment of it, he would tell me in great sensual detail what it felt like to fly through the bright air before the chute kicked in, the sounds, the sight, the touch of the sky as he fell through it down towards the waiting earth.

Every moment. Every moment.

Every second he spent in the blue was a lived one, a treasured one. The sky belonged to him, and he to it.

Putting that free spirit into the ground would have been a crime. I had not made a promise, as such, but I knew that I had made a promise nonetheless. He would have his last jump. From the instant that his ashes arrived back into his home, I knew that this would have to be the send-off that he would have wanted, that he deserved. There would be no 'funeral'. Just a last flight.

I looked at options—perhaps there could be a way I could hire someone to fly me up in a small plane or a helicopter and I could pour out his ashes up there myself. Or maybe I could go up in hot air balloon ride, and likewise. But I always knew that the best way—the way that would most honour him, and his memory—would be if I could find a skydiving club with someone willing to make that jump—to share the last jump that Deck would make—to scatter his ashes up there for me while coming back down to earth in that silence that he once wrote about (so uncharacteristically eloquently—he was a reporter, not a poet, and such language did not come easily to him).

When I first contacted the Snohomish Skydive club about this, I spoke to a woman with whom I shared some of those stories (she laughed and laughed at the watermelon tale…) and she asked me perfectly sincerely, not knowing me and what I was, whether I had considered "writing these down somewhere to share with people". But she took my details and she said one of the club's officers would be in touch with me. One of them did, phoning me back to tell me that that they did do this sort of thing occasionally and that they would be honoured to participate in sending a brother skydiver to his final rest. That was in April. I said I wanted to arrange for this to happen as close to July 13th as possible—because that would have been our 21st wedding anniversary. I was told that this could be arranged, and that I should phone back closer to the time to nail down arrangements.

I called back when summer came knocking, and spoke to a different person at the club—and it was with him that I made the final disposition of events. They wouldn't be doing any jumping on the 13th—but the 14th would be a go, with the proviso that I should phone on the day of the jump just to make sure that the weather would cooperate.

I did. The weather did. I picked up Deck's skydiving credentials—that typewritten account that he wrote of his first jump, a newspaper clipping from one of the times he landed in trouble from a jump, and one surviving ass-over-teakettle photo which may have been of that first jump showing a human figure barreling down head first with legs in a frantic V and his rear pointed at the heavens—and gathered up the urn with his ashes which had been sitting on his desk in the downstairs office, behind me, since it came home back in February—and he left home for the last time.

I talked to him, all the way. I locked the door and stepped out to the car and turned, with the urn in hand, and told him to look at his house one last time, to say his farewells. I got into the car and drove out the back way through the woods, the road he loved, and across the bridge that they had taken a year to rebuild when the old one became too unsafe for traffic—and asked him if he remembered that mess, and to wave goodbye to the (now not so new) bridge as we drove over it. I turned onto the road which I drove while he was at the Sedro Woolley hospital facility, which was supposed to take me to Hwy 9 which I would take all the way to Snohomish—but my driving instructions from the computer and my GPS had different ideas (the GPS insisted on the I-5…) and I took a wrong turning or three somewhere, ended up driving straight past that hospital facility (which I hadn't intended to do—but told him about it, and told him to wave goodbye to that, too, because that was the place where he "died" first, where they resuscitated him back on December 7, before sending him off to Bellingham's main hospital where his journey to the end began). And then after another wrong turn I gave up and let the GPS take me to the freeway, and just drove down to Snohomish directly, fast, without the scenic "back road" option I had planned on taking.

The sky was blue. Very blue. I was so aware of it as I was driving. The sky part of which he would soon become. I told him over and over again how blue the sky was today. His urn sat on the passenger seat, where he would have been sitting if he'd been traveling with me—silent presence—I complained at it that he was napping again, as he was wont to do on lengthy drives when I really wanted him to chirp up and talk at me and keep me entertained while I drove. But this sleep was deeper. He did not wake. He could not wake. He would never talk again.

Because I had allowed for more time (anticipating the back roads) I got to my destination sooner than I had planned—but my friend Mir, who had known both Deck and me for decades and whom I had called for moral support, was already there to meet me. Conversations with the club people had already been had—everyone was waiting for me. Mir asked if assistance was required with carrying either the folder I had all the ephemera in or the urn with the ashes, but I hung onto both. Today was not a day I wanted to let go of Deck, not before I had to, not until they had to take him out back where they would decant the ashes into several canisters which could be taken aloft and from which the ashes could be safely poured. I met Tyson, the guy I'd arranged all this with over the phone, and he told me how things would go—the flight that would take up Brent, the skydiver who was going to do the jump, would go aloft sometime between 3 and 3:15, and several other hops carrying student skydivers would precede it, and I could watch those jumps as they happened to give me an idea—but when Deck's flight went up someone would come out to the shaded observation area to help point out where to look when Brent jumped.

Mir wanted to know when was the last time I'd had any water and I admitted to not being properly hydrated.

"You're wobbling," Mir said. "You need to drink water. You need to keep drinking water."

A water bottle was procured, with the Snohomish Skydiver logo. I was instructed to keep chugging from it and to refill when necessary.

Brent, the skydiver who would do the jump, came out

to meet me, and I gave him a copy of one of my books (the "Untranslatable" collection of stories) and a copy of that first-jump article that Deck wrote. He sat down and read it, clearly affected by it.

"Is there anything you want me to say, up there?" he asked.

"I'll write it down for you," I said, and on a piece of paper I tore from a notebook in my bag I wrote Delenn's words from Babylon 5: "If I do not see you again here, I will see you once more in that place where no shadows fall." It was a show Deck and I both loved. He would know the line. He would know exactly where it came from. It was a final shared word in a shared world. It would be released in the sky with him, halfway to the stars that we both loved.

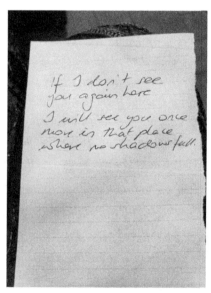

And then it was a matter of waiting. And then the plane that would take him up taxied up to the observation area. I took a couple of photos, of the plane, of the jumper

carrying the canisters which were all that remained of Deck, and I took a video of the plane taxiing out, gaining speed on the runway of the airfield, taking to the skies. And then someone came out to us.

"You're here for the ash dive?"

I nodded.

"He'll come out first, before the rest of them—right above."

I looked up into the blue, blue sky. Brent's chute was called, appropriately, "Infinity" (I took a photo of THAT, while he was waiting to go up) and it was blue, like the sky, and when someone first called out, "there it is", and pointed at the sky at first I could not see anything at all except that all-encompassing blue—and then a speck of sky separated out and became a discrete thing, and I could see the blue chute starting to descend.

Brent emptied the first canister way high—at 8000 feet—and we did not see that. But the two he poured out lower down—we could see the ash scatter, we could see the silver arc of it follow him across the sky as he spiraled down towards us.

I was amazingly calm. I was clear-eyed. I was not crying, although there was a silence inside of me, that silence that Deck spoke of in his account, the silence of the jump which I now shared with him as he became part of air and brightness all around me. Brent came down, and I took a video of that. And then he collected the sky blue parachute and came back into the club.

He'd taken video. They'd send it to me. They took my

*email address. I said thank you. Again. And again. And
again. The tears were waiting, but they did not really come.
Not yet. They were an ocean deep within me.*

*Mir and I walked away from the club, past what I
said were "stables" for airplanes—structures which housed
parked small planes, Cessnas and Piper Cubs, some with
'blindfolds' over their cockpit windows, staked down. Small
planes, Deck's delight, ever since the Stinson he briefly
owned and flew himself—he was always in love with air,
with wings.*

*"He would have LOVED this," I said, my voice
catching a little, looking at the planes which he would have
taken such joy in. "I can almost see his eyes shining…"*

"They are," Mir said.

*And in a way that was perfectly true. Deck was
right there—everywhere—beside me, around me, above
me—and yes, those eyes were shining. He might not have
been a bona fide haint, a ghost drifting along in my wake,
but he was present, his joy was present, the shine in those
eyes was there. This was one of those things, one of those
MOMENTS he held so beloved.*

*That, I could give him. The last thing I could give
him. The sky. The joy. That last moment.*

*It was making good on a promise I had made in my
heart.*

*Mir insisted I eat something before I started back—
and again, I was preternaturally calm. The way I described
it to Mir was that I was sort of miserably happy, and
that about covers it. I had done what needed to be done
but I was here right now in what was a parting, a time
to say goodbye. I had given him into gentle hands, and a*

parachute called Infinity unfurled above him as all that remained of his physical body now became part of my memories, of that particular shade of sky blue, of a gentle rumble of a small plane engine gearing up to take flight, of a rustle of those wings which he folded around me to keep me safe twenty one years ago and in whose protection I had lived for a couple of decades. A couple of decades of a shared lifetime. He once gave me a card that said "I will always love you"—but forever doesn't last as long as it used to—mine lasted for twenty years, six months, and eighteen days, and it ended up—as it had to end, given who Deck was—in that moment in which nothing existed but him and me and the life we had built together and the instant of saying goodbye.

I made my way home, still numb, still dry. And it was only when I got here, and closed the door of my home behind me, entering into the place where he would never be again, that I broke down, and cried helplessly for an hour. But those were, for the first time, tears that didn't taste wholly of bitterest grief. They tasted of light. And of sky. And of a release of a bright, bright spirit.

That was a moment I could take, and treasure. That was a moment that will always stay with me, that will always be mine. He will be in every sky now, in every silence. In every moment.

Fly, my love. I set you free, in that eternal moment. In the light. In that open sky, where you have always belonged.

And I will see you again… in that place where no shadows fall.

☙

THE HOSPICE PEOPLE OFFERED TO make me a bear out of one of Deck's shirts, and they did that, and what I called the "uglibear" (he won't win any beauty contests, but he is a darling) is living on the bed now, beside Deck's pillow. And I suddenly knew that I might give all of Deck's stuff away eventually—but not those flannel plaid shirts which were so much the essence of him. So they came back for the rest of the shirts, and they made me a small memory-quilt throw from them.

I keep it folded on the bed beside me. It foolishly feels like he is kind of sort of there, in the shape of that.

I carried on writing updates.

Ↄ⁓

29 July 2021 (my blog)

> *It's weird, but grieving is… waiting. It's waiting for the minutes to add up to an hour, for hours to add up to a day, for days to string together like pearls. I'm not sure what the waiting is FOR. The worst that can happen has happened already, hasn't it, the thing that triggered the grieving in the first place, so what are we waiting for? For the automagical moment of "it's all better now" that never comes? Or just for the time to pass, letting the scab harden on the wound?*

> *I had a meltdown yesterday triggered by a STUPID little snip of memory which I am not even sure where it came from at all—the memory of taking Deck to the blood coagulation clinic where he went to have his meds monitored (he was on blood thinners, and they had a certain bracket of Numbers they wished his levels to be at and this had to be checked every eight weeks or so, except in wintertimes when I wussed out and wouldn't drive in icy circumstances and the boat got pushed out to longer breaks so I could snatch at a quick moment of good weather*

*in which to whip him over there and back...) We'd get
there, and we'd always have to go through the exact same
song and dance—"everything still the same? still living
at the same address? all insurances identical to those that
were in place eight weeks ago? yes, you can sign for him on
the electronic thingy... now write down your relationship
to... oh, you've already done it... ok you're all set..." and
then we would go and park ourselves on the waiting room
chairs and wait for the call for "Robert" (a name which
always startled both of us because he NEVER went by his
full moniker...) and the retreat back into the surgery rooms
for literally five minutes at a time—look up profile on
computer, prick his finger, get a drop of blood, stick it into
the reader machine, note the number that pops up, you're
fine, thank you for coming, see you in eight weeks.*

     *It was a boondoggle and an annoyance which he kept
on grumbling about because the script never varied and
he was always patted onna head and sent on his way after*

that five-minute interaction which took a half-hour drive there and a half-hour drive back (and no, during the worst of the pandemic we simply DID NOT GO AT ALL. it was not worth the potential risk for what did not seem to be a really DRASTIC need). But now... now... I think back on that, and I think I would give almost anything to have him here, to make sure he had all the necessary "spare parts" on hand (the hearing aid, the cane... the weight he wore on his bad arm, to keep it down... helping him on with the shoe with the leg brace on it...), to load him into the car, to drive him somewhere while he remarked on how pretty the lake looked that day, to have him hand me his glasses to clean when we got to the waiting room, to share some stupid little thing from the New Yorker or the Time magazine or even some celebrity gossip rag languishing there on the waiting room tables. To hear him laugh. To see him make his slow careful way back to the car from the clinic, or to run on ahead (if I had to park too far) and bring the car so that he wouldn't have to traipse the length of the parking lot to get there.

I cried myself empty over the loss of that stupid, stupid, stupid little waiting room, and the lost waiting times that unfolded within it. Because THAT waiting was a wait for something shared to come, and to go, and a return to something else shared when we got home from it. Now I am alone in God's waiting room, waiting to hear his name called, and will never hear it called again. I was waiting for something, then. I am waiting for nothing, now, and yet I am still waiting. And that solitary vigil is a long-term thing. I will be... sitting in this waiting room for a long time.

They say grief is the price you pay for love. Ah, but love is expensive...

Photo by Greg Rosenke on Unsplash

☙

1 August 2021

Dear love, it's six months. SIX MONTHS. I'm still here and you could say I'm surviving—but I'm treading water, and trying to remember whether I am still able to swim. I know there's no bottom beneath me, just the abyss, and the abyss is full of monsters, and I'm a long way from where I'm able to think about putting my feet down and feeling solid ground. It's been "apres toi le deluge"—I've been flooded out, hanging onto flotsam to stay afloat, living minute by minute. Hour by hour. Day by day. There are still times when everything just grinds to a halt and time itself stands still and I find myself frozen in the moment— and it doesn't seem to matter what I just finished doing, or what I am supposed to do next. Sometimes it comes in the mornings, when it becomes hard to imagine why on earth I would want to get up.

Sometimes it manifests in the middle of the day and I'm staring mindlessly at the computer screen, with no more brain room than to scroll aimlessly through Facebook. Sometimes I look at the clock and at the day fading into shadow beside me and wonder dispassionately if that means it might be "dinner time" although I don't feel particularly hungry or take any particular pleasure in any particular food. I have bought edible things which have sat in the fridge for too long and became... less than edible... I cannot seem to *plan* anything. It's a question of living moment by moment, hour by hour, day by day.

And, it seems, month by month. I am aware that as of this moment I have already lived one fortieth of the time

I got to spend with you and that the clock is ticking—and that every second that passes takes me further away from you. What will happen to me when I reach a year without you, or ten years without you... I don't even know yet. I know a part of me is letting you go. I also know there's a part of me that's clinging desperately on—that this piece of floating debris in this endless ocean that's the only thing that is keeping me afloat... is the memory of you.

I miss you.

ဆာ

4 August 2021

I overslept this morning - possibly because I didn't get to SLEEP AT ALL until 3 AM. Either way, I was still asleep when the phone rang this morning and woke me out of a dream I did not did not did not want to leave.

Deck was sitting in his chair in the living room and I had brought up a snippet of story for him to read—a new thing, very possibly a new novel, I had a glimpse into the "story" itself and it was a convoluted complicated plotline—and it was night time, dark outside, the TV on, and he smiled at me and said, "now now—not TONIGHT! It's way too late to start this. I'll look at it in the morning—you'll have it when you wake up." (that was our thing—you'll have it when you wake up meant that he would as usual be up with the roosters and mucking about on his computer at 4 AM, HOURS before I stirred, and he'd get stuff done in those quiet hours...) And I play-whined, as I often did when it came to these stories, "but now! I want you to look at it now! I don't want you to edit it I just want a reaction—and you can do anything further tomorrow when you..." And he sighed and said, "okay, read it to me"…

…and then the phone rang.

I usually call my mom every morning when I wake up—but this morning I OVERSLEPT and she decided to take matters into her own hands and call me to find out "if I was all right".

No, I am not all right. This was the first time—that I remember—that I dreamed of Deck since he left me. And I might have wished to be allowed to wake from it properly, to leave it gently, not to have it torn from me, popped like a soap bubble, so that now I am struggling to remember it at all.

Damn it.

ᥱᳱ

14 August 2021 (my blog)

You all probably know full well the so-called five stages of grief: **denial and isolation, anger, bargaining, depression, and acceptance.** *But what fails to be understood, generally, is that it not as linear as it is stated, it's (at best) a spiral, and you find yourself going back and forth all the time bouncing between stages you could have sworn you'd already gone through but dang, there you are, hello, I recognise this road, this signpost, I've been here before, haven't I?*

I go through micro-denials all the time. I find myself lying in bed at night with my eyes closed but not yet asleep, and my thoughts will drift to some form of "he is gone", and my entire body will jerk instinctively into a sharp "NO!" before I have a chance to stop it. It's denial upon denial upon denial and I have no brakes on that train at all, it just keeps circling back to bite me.

Anger? I stand in my kitchen, alone, the kitchen that was "his" kitchen because he dealt with the cooking, and I look at a pot which I have to fill with something because I am still alive and I have to eat or I won't be much longer, and there's a limp sort of fury that stabs at me—"how could you leave me alone with a lifetime of cooking for one stretching out in front of me?"

Bargaining? I tried that. God wasn't having any of it.

Depression? Hellfire yes. I'm borderline clinical. I cry at the drop of a hat. I am triggered by stupid things, by something I glimpse on a TV show which never used to matter before—some TV shows I can't watch at all because they were "our" shows and I can't bear to watch them without him. I still haven't seen the new Leverage series mostly because I went there to look and the first scenes were WIDOWHOOD and I just couldn't hack it. I go to bed crying. I wake up crying. At some point it's gotta get better because I'll dehydrate myself right outta tears at this rate. But depression? oh yeah. it lives here now.

And acceptance? Sorry, I don't think I'll ever get there. I cannot accept this. I just bounce off it when I try.

Maybe I'll just end up being depressed enough to grow numb, and that will do in lieu of acceptance.

In the meantime, I am trying to stay remotely productive. I am editing a MS for publication soon (it's in the proofreading/formatting stages now so it's a lot of hurry up and wait while other people do their thing). I even went out on a limb and submitted a couple of short stories to various places recently. Who knows, right? But I haven't written any new fiction for six months, barring one short story which even I can tell is more of a cri de coeur than anything literarily brilliant in any way—and of course it's the first story that my in-house editor that I had for twenty years did not see and "fix" before I could show it to other people. I mean, I wrote before I met Deck and I can probably write again at some point but for those twenty shared years *he was part of the process* and now I have to learn to write all over again.

Stages of grief? I'm in all of them, all at once.

It's been just over six months since I became a widow. I simultaneously cannot believe that it's been so short, and that it's been so long. I think I have barely stirred from the start line, and there's a marathon waiting to be run—and the stages of grief are waiting for me at every step I take forward, like so many traps just yawning for me. I guess the only acceptance I can muster right now is basically the acceptance that I am Frodo Baggins—I am wounded, wounded, and I will never really heal—not until I find the twilit quays where waits a ship to bear me to the uttermost west.

I will write about more cheerful stuff soon. I promise.

19 August 2021

Tonight I ran out of time.

Many years ago—back in the early years of this century—I was actually at a convention (Wiscon, as it happens—I remember this vividly) when the watch I was wearing then simply DIED and no amount of poking or prodding—on my own behalf or by the jeweller to whom I took it to see if they could wake it up—did the trick.

That one was well and truly RIP—which left me in a quandary—yes I know everyone carries around a cell phone NOW and relies on that for the time but even that was not QUITE so ubiquitous back then and anyway I did not have one—to tell the time I needed a quick glance at my wrist.

So I bought a new watch, in that jeweller in Madison. It happened to be a very good brand but it also happened to be offered at somewhat heavy discount and that seemed like a good deal to snap up. It had a metal link bracelet, though, which had to be resized to fit my skinny wrist (otherwise the watch would just dangle there, or else sit halfway up my arm...)

This thing has been on my wrist for damn near two decades now, patiently ticking away.

Tonight, it just stopped. I didn't even realise it immediately but when I did glance down, at some point during the evening, it was very clear that the time I was seeing was NOT the time that I was actually living in. (there must be a story in here somewhere...) I'm going to take it in to be disemboweled in the hope that it might still be as simple as replacing a battery. But if not...

if not...

tonight is a metaphor rising.

Tonight i ran out of time. The clock ran out on the life I had been living, finally and unequivocally. I am living in the interstices now until I can kickstart the clock again.

Or be told that time past, time stopped, cannot be rekindled. Ever.

I am not sure I am ready for this.

UPDATE for those following along at home:

Took it to a jeweller's which advertised that they dealt with that brand of watch. Oh sure we can check the battery, they said, and then tried to root around in order to get the back off the watch to get into the battery, and then came back to me and said, sorry, these things usually have a little 'lip' on the edge where our tool can catch and then we can lift the cover off but your watch doesn't seem to have one—and we don't have the tools—but there's this dedicated clock repair place literally round the corner from there (what are the odds?) and so I picked up my broken little timepiece and took it over to the watch doctor.

The tiny shop is packed with those old fashioned floor-standing grandfather clocks—I don't think I've seen one more than once or twice in my lifetime and here there were a baker's dozen standing there and ticking away quietly in their best noble grandfather clock manner—and I go to talk to the guy who runs the place who has receding graying hair and spectacles on a lanyard around his neck and honestly the whole place is a setting for a fairy story about fae that meddle with time, lock, stock, and proprietor... Anyway. He looks at the watch, changes the battery, and finds that it is still stone dead. The possible solution is to "put a new movement in".

Oh my friends. The metaphor thickens.

The watch is there now, awaiting a rebirth of time once the movement gets replaced. Either way, I think that I am being bludgeoned upside the head with a clue-by-four. The past is dead and gone. It's either long live the future or it all ends here.

ॐ

23 August 2021

Just when you think you might have passed a hump you realise you're in a trench on the other side. I've been having a two-day crying jag that doesn't seem to show any signs of stopping. I feel like a house with a broken window and a hurricane is blowing in. Every time I try to STOP THINKING something else finds a chink and flies inside and takes the roof off all over again.

My heart hurts. Literally. Like someone has got it in a merciless fist and is squeezing it.

My eyes hurt. My TEARS hurt, it's like I'm oozing acid.

I'm sorry, I don't know how to get past this.

I wrote this message and erased it twice because it feels like I'm just a wet dishrag dripping on everyone's screens. I'm sorry. it's just that I've never felt this alone before.

ை

6 September 2021

This is what I used to wake up to every morning: a cup of coffee, a square of chocolate, and a shared precious moment while I consumed these, often still webbed in dreams which I could share with someone who didn't always comprehend them but always accepted them and even helped me turn some of them into stories. I woke every morning... to love. Yes, I was spoiled like that for twenty years (barring only a few months when he was physically unable to carry a coffee cup, in the immediate aftermath of his stroke).

Today I took a square of chocolate... and sobbed over it for an hour because those mornings rose to haunt me like an army of sorrowful spirits. I suddenly remembered them with a senseless clarity, a memory with diamond edges cutting into my soul.

There is this cloud, all around me. Grey and shapeless and formless and eternal. I think I live here now.

☙

14 September 2021

When I was very young and we first moved to Africa, I ended up in a convent school (although I was not Catholic, which blew the nuns' minds—but it was the best school my parents could find for me so off I went...) I can still rattle off a Hail Mary at the drop of a hat even though I wasn't really required as a non-Catholic to participate in direct prayers or in Mass—but the school chapel was EXTREMELY Catholic, down to individual panels on the sides of the building depicting the Stations of the Cross. It wasn't as though I was REQUIRED to learn them (Catholic catechism being something I was excused from) but it's hard not to osmose stuff like this when you're surrounded by it like some exotic extraterrestrial atmosphere. Two years there, and by the end of it I could have "passed" as a good little Catholic schoolgirl if pushed.

Most of it's gone now (except for the Hail Mary) but the reason I bring this up is those Stations of the Cross—because right now that's what life feels like, I am crawling along some holy wall looking at pictures and figuring out where on that journey I currently am. At this precise moment I am fighting the notion that everything is "temporary", that I am simply in stasis, waiting for something, for something to end, for something else to begin. Because this life, the one I am currently in, doesn't seem real. I'm biding my time. I'm treading water. I'm hanging in space with my tether snapped and my world a long way below me and nothing above me but hostile airless dark (it's pretty to be sure and it is as always full of distant stars but right now they don't seem... exactly... relevant...)

I am looking into the fridge and thinking, "I need eggs" and then thinking, "I'll deal with that tomorrow... or maybe the next day". I'm looking at the weather forecast and it's turning cool and maybe the heater will be required and I'm thinking, "I can't decide on whether not I'm cold. I may have been. Or maybe I will be. I will think about that later". Things like that. Mostly I am looking into a future which seems nothing but fog and shadow, a future in which absolutely nothing is possible to make actual plans about, but at the same time a future into which I am shoving stuff because I don't seem to be capable of thinking straight about anything long term—as in, I'll just put this HERE and look at it LATER even though a part of me doesn't believe in LATER any more so I can't justify that thought and that decision at all. I'm looking at "this is my life" and trying to grapple with the possibility that "this is the rest of my life" and every now and then I just go ice cold, and then I internally combust until I feel my skin flushing with heat, and none of it has to do with whether or not I have turned the heater on or off or formed any intention to do either. It's that black hole at the center, sucking at my insides, every now and then lurching my heart into a full stop before it instinctively and obstinately starts beating again.

Simple things like scheduling a blog post stymie me now (I flubbed that, twice, in the last couple of weeks). I am left wondering which station of the cross this is, this state of confusion, and what, if anything at all, follows it.

What do I have to hold onto, or abandon, to take those next steps? Do I even remember how to walk...?

ℰℬ

29 September 2021 (my blog)

Someday soon I might find the right words to think about other things. Until then... stuff like this comes out.

Bear with me.

Or scroll by.

A Day in the Life

9 AM
Cats want breakfast. Drag self out of bed.
Debate whether or not I woke up with a headache.
Feed cats. Make sure they have water.
Fifteen hours left to fill.

10 AM
Put the recycling together, take it out to kerbside.
Clean litter boxes, put in trash bag,
take out the garbage to the bin. Drag to kerbside.
Come in, wash hands. Consider breakfast. Decline.
Make first cup of coffee.
Fourteen hours left to fill.

11AM
Consider putting heat on (it's Fall). Decide against it –
the sun is out, it feels extravagant.
Share a weird Facebook post with anyone who might be reading.
Thirteen hours left to fill.

12 PM
There's an email that needs answering. Begin that.

There's an interview that needs doing. Begin that.
Finish nothing.
Twelve hours left to fill.

1PM
Leaves are falling. Remember how we used to talk about
shuffling through them.
Together. A thing shared.
Watch leaves falling, alone, for a while.
Hypnotic.
Think about the symbolism of letting go.
Eleven hours left to fill.

2 PM
Consider going for a walk, but hip hurts today.
I've abandoned ideas for less.
Think about a couple of bills I wrote checks for yesterday
can't find the envelopes. Did I mail them already?
can't remember.
Ten hours left to fill.

3PM
More coffee. Back to Facebook, and checking things out
on the rest of the internet.
Try again with the interview. Don't finish. First have to
find
something interesting to talk about.
Remember some random thing about last year.
Cry quietly.
Nine hours left to fill.

4PM
Watch squirrels chase each other outside.
This morning there was one at the kitchen window,
looking in hopefully. Thought about feeding it.
Didn't quite make it there. Remember this.

Consider going out to feed them now.
Let the thought slide away.
Keep watching the squirrels play.
Eight hours left to fill.

    5PM
This is about the time HE usually said,
'Oops, I'd better do something about supper'.
Consider the idea. Think about alternatives.
Pizza? Perhaps… I'll just have mac & cheese.
I know I am not eating right.
At least I had spinach two days ago.
Seven hours left to fill.

    6PM
Throw together some pasta, eat in front of the TV.
For God's sake, I am watching; 'Baywatch'.
There is no hope. (but at least it isn't something
we both loved. It doesn't trigger me. And the drama
is so transparently fake that it is easy to bear.)
Six hours left to fill.

    7PM
The days are definitely shorter. It's getting darker.
'Baywatch' still on TV (double episode). Mindlessly playing
cards
while those moving pictures move—
laying out a patience—asking it a question—
'will I be OK?'—the cards deny it.
Five hours left to fill.

    8PM
Full dark outside.
TV switches to Star Trek TOS. I know
most of these episodes by heart. I can
mouth the dialogue as it is spoken.

This takes up space in my head.
Knitting a scarf in progress; pick up the knitting.
It helps if hands are busy.
Cats asleep beside me.
Silence, other than for the echo of the familiar dialogue.
Four hours left to fill.

9PM
TV switches to Star Trek TNG. Keep watching.
Keep knitting. The cats are still sleeping.
Wake them and shed them, to make myself some tea,
the kind that might help me sleep later. Eventually.
It has chamomile in it. And some other stuff that is
supposed to bring sleep.
Eventually.
Three hours left to fill.

10PM
TV now on Star Trek DS9. Again, I've seen all of these
episodes.
But I am still sitting here, still knitting the scarf. It has
lengthened.
At least there is that.
At some point I get up in a surge of guilt and energy
and go back to the computer to see if anything important
has happened.
Nothing new. Other people's lives continue.
I look at my reflection in the window beside me
and wonder about my own.
Two hours left to fill.

11PM
The silence is absolute. TV'd out.
Don't want to knit any more.
Give cats an evening snack.
Consider an aspirin (hip hurts. head hurts. heart hurts.)

Take one. Have misgivings. Too late.
One hour left to fill.

    12AM

Go to bed. Get up once because fire alarm is chirping.
Take battery out. Have to deal with that in the morning.
Maybe.
Try to read for a while
Maybe it's the book. I can't keep my focus.
Switch off the light and say, though you can't hear me,
'Good Night, I love you'
like I've done every night for twenty years spent with you.
Silence responds. Silence remains.

    It's past midnight, and I lie in the dark
awake
on the bedside clock the hours drift by.

    1AM

    2AM

    3AM

    At some point I'll close my eyes and pass out
maybe dream strange dreams
the kind I used to tell you about
in the mornings
when you brought in my coffee
and a piece of chocolate tucked into an old saved pocket for
a teabag,
against melting in your hand.
In the mornings
which are gone.
Empty of you.
One is coming again, soon.

    8AM, I am awake.

9AM, cats want breakfast.

Another day to fill.

❦

3 October 2021

Dear love, today I did something very brave or very stupid or possibly both.

I went back to the Fork, with a friend. First time in many months.

First time since... since YOU.

There were many times we went there and WANTED this table, our table, but it was taken or reserved, and we ended up drifting somewhere in the middle... but this time... it was like it was waiting there for me to come in. They took us straight there. It hit me like a gut punch. My friend sat where you usually sat, and looking across the table and seeing her face and not yours was shocking. I sat with my eyes full of tears. We talked about stuff—I don't remember what.

"You aren't here," she said to me at one point.

But I was. I WAS. Too much of me was here. Too many ghosts. And speaking of ghosts... the background music suddenly changed to Gershwin, and the soulful notes of 'someone to watch over me' began to drift through the room. And I just curled up into a ball and stuffed my hands into my eye sockets and said, "I MISS YOU SO MUCH"

My friend just sat there and looked at me sadly.

I finished my breakfast. We got up to go. And the music changed again just as we were leaving. "Oh.... my

*love... my darling... I hunger for your touch... a long lonely
time... and time goes by so slowly and time can mean so
much... are you still mine...?"*

*I waited until I got home, I managed that much. But
I've been sobbing ever since I closed my front door.*

It's been eight months since you left me.

Are you still mine...?

℘

*5 October 2021—Looking for a Re-set Button (my
blog)*

*I find myself blundering about on the internet, doing
nothing much in particular. I waste time on stupid social
media memes, scrolling down the newsfeed of things like
Facebook, obsessively checking email as though I am
expecting some notification (I am not). I am wrestling the
recalcitrant minutes into submission, making them pass. I
am not sure what day it is; checking the calendar is often
useless because I find my eyes swimming in the dates not
knowing which is today and which was two days ago. I
have taken to crossing off each day on the kitchen calendar
when I get up in the mornings, just so that I can keep
myself from coming unstuck in time.*

*I have no idea what I am looking for, on the net, in
the emails. Some sort of a reset button, something that I
can find and recognise and press, and then when I go back
upstairs life will be normal again, and Deck will be sitting
at his computer, and there would be supper to fix for the
both of us when the sun goes down, and then there would
be an hour or two of often mindless shared television—it
didn't matter what we were watching so much as we were*

watching it together (well it DID matter—we didn't watch drivel—but you know what I mean.)

I am looking for a reset button to press so that I can stop being ambushed by crying jags, so that I can stop pausing as I walk past his office and glancing at the empty chair, so that I can stop switching off the living room lamp and dragging myself to bed in darkness whispering "good night I love you" into the silence as though he can hear me. I am looking for a reset button. I want my life back.

Things are about to unravel dramatically, in another month or so. Mid November marks the moment that he left home… and never returned. Early December marks the one year anniversary of his first death, the time his heart stopped in the little country hospital, the place they clawed him back from the brink; the rest of December marks increasingly desperate procedures, stents, pacemaker, drains… and then, just before Christmas, the Covid axe that fell when they moved him to the nursing home and separated us, for the last time, for good. January, in the nursing home; the return to the hospital; the beginning of the end; the night of the hospice; the last wet dreary rainy hours of pre-dawn on February 1. Getting up in a world where he no longer existed.

November marks the beginning of the first anniversary of all that.

It is coming up to a year.

I cannot believe that. He can't have been gone for a year. I can't have already lived alone one twentieth of the time that we had spent together. It just cannot be.

I want a reset button. I want to wake up and find him there.

It can't be nearly a year. It can't. It can't.

Things fall apart. The center cannot hold.

I want a reset.

෬

The Dark Road (first appeared on Medium)

I chronicled the last journey of my beloved, right until the end. And social media has a long memory. I woke up shaking on December 7 because that was the day on which he first "died", when his heart stopped and they brought him back via some difficult CPR which left him in pain for a long time afterwards (they may have cracked ribs) and delivered him into his final two months of being alive, two months of medical hell. In those two months he would spend weeks in the ICU (at least once unconscious and intubated), undergoing two surgical procedures to clear clogged arteries, one of those procedures went bad (perforated artery, bleeding into the pericardium, chest drains, the works) and the insertion of a pacemaker - and then he would get turfed into a nursing home for "rehabilitation and therapy" which only happened intermittently if it happened at all because futzing around with his medications often produced blood coag levels that indicated that his blood was the thickness of water and if anyone touched him too hard he would bleed out on the spot. And then other medical issues grew, there in the home, and then he was turfed back into hospital… where, right until the final twenty four hours or so, he was still speaking valiantly of "coming home".

He never did.

In the dark after-midnight hours of February 1 he

slipped away for good.

And left me holding a tattered map, of love and memory.

I am not entirely sure where I am now, metaphorically speaking. The map is rudimentary, hand-drawn, fading, incomplete. All I can tell you is that I am somewhere on a desolate plain, winds howling around me and no shelter to be had, the ground cracked and dry at my feet and what vegetation there is brittle and stunted and a deathly brownish gray that couldn't possibly ever have been green and growing. If I look up, the sky is a milky gray with a diluted light which might be daylight or the fading of the day, it's hard to tell, there is no actual sun to show it. Everything has two shadows, anyway. In front of me there seems to be nothing - just more desolate plain - the map is unhelpful on the matter.. Behind me... oh, I turn around and I see them there. The dark hills.

I have a memory of the country beyond those dark hills. There are valleys snaking up between them, and paths, and they lead to a place where the sun spills over green slopes, and wild flowers grow on them, and bright streams tumble through them. I can see wings in the sky where birds are flying. I can see tracks were deer have passed. The place is alive with life and joy. There is a presence there - a companionship - and it is in that companionship that all these pieces of life and joy are rooted. I remember laughter. I remember days spent in shared labors, and then evenings of rest in one another. I remember firelight in the night, mulled cider in mugs warm to the touch of hands wrapped around them, finishing each other's sentences, constantly surprised by the way each of us complemented and fulfilled the other. I remember...

...that's what the map is showing me. An image of that lost and lovely place now gone forever. Because when he left the light closed in the heavens above. The meadows on the slopes darkened; the brooks became peaty and slow and then disappeared into the ground. I could see no trace of bird or beast, or the hearth in which our fires burned. The hills darkened, and closed in around me, and I walked, and the hills spat me out onto this plain at last. I can turn and look at them but they are shut now, a barrier and not a path, and the paradise they once held has been gathered up and swept away. The map tells me where it had been - but even if I could retrace my steps and go back precisely to where the x marks the spot on the map I know I will find no such place in what is my new reality. This is a map to memory. And what it remembers is no more.

There are dark paths through those dark hills. The wind is blowing and the night is still coming and I am alone on that windy plain and the earth is broken under my feet, a parched and cracked earth which has not seen water for an age, which is itself a memory, now turning into dust. The dark hills are a wall behind me, a wall that hides things that I am finding it difficult to believe ever realy existed, that seem to me now to have been a beautiful dream - and if it weren't for the scrap of map, here in my hand, I could believe that I have always stood in the desert of this empty plain, that there was never anything else, that this is not a new thing but an old one and I have just woken back into it from the warmth of that dream that I had, the dream where I loved and was loved in return. Love is the soft rain that fed those meadows, those flowers, those birds and those beasts, ourselves. And love is gone now.

The place where love lived is gone now.

*And between me and even the memory of it, now…
those dark hills. High and shadowed and forbidding. If
there had been a path there at all it is gone now, swept
away. There is no going back - no road, and no purpose.
But what lies ahead leaves me bone weary just to look upon
it. It is an endless trudge in an endless pale twilight that is
neither night nor day, a misery of parched mourning, with
the dark hills always and forever a reminder and a sweet
poison in my mind.*

*I have a feeling that no matter how far and how long
I walk on this plain, if I should turn at any time there they
will be, the dark hills, no further away than they are right
now. They move with me, and follow me, the ramparts that
sunder me from the memory of love, mocking me with their
lost roads and lost light and lost happiness.*

*Alone on the darkling plain, I carry the dark hills
within me.*

❧

It may not have been the best timing to choose but I was perhaps looking for places that echoed my own grieving, and I read
two books in recent months that I had known of but had never
read before—and maybe had not been equipped to read before.
One of them was C S Lewis's slim volume, *A Grief Observed*,
thoughts on the loss of his beloved wife less than a handful of
years into their marriage. The other was Joan Didion's *The Year of
Magical Thinking*, in her case a searing account of the aftermath
of the loss of a mate of more than forty years. The takeaway is
that grief is grief, and there are parts of both books which I can,
possibly, only now fully understand. My copy of Didion is dog-
eared whenever I found a particular instance that tore into me,
that I recognized. I was another such left-behind wife, another
widow, and what she says resonates with me, sometimes violent-

ly. I read the book and sobbed. There are many MANY dog-eared pages. I could spend quite some time giving you the quotes that touched me, the truths I recognised, but it wouldn't matter—if you aren't here, with me, with her, with us, if you aren't part of this tribe yet, then you don't yet deserve to be plunged into that maelstrom ahead of time, to be invited inside ahead of your own hour, you will not completely understand; and if you are… then I do not need to tell you about any of it. You already know.

This is a peculiar state of mind—I mean, you are kind of born into a world which consists of generations. It is understood and accepted that those generations which came before you will also leave before you. I grieved bitterly the loss of my beloved grandparents, but that was more than thirty years ago now. That grief is wrapped in memory now, and while I still miss my grandmother to the day and always will… she died way too young, anyway… it was not exactly unexpected. One is prepared for that. When my father died (the first of HIS generation in my life, the beginning of that crumbling) I mourned him—I missed him (I still do)—I hold him in memory yet green, but yet again, this was a generational thing. At some point I will lose my last remaining parent and become truly one for the "widows and orphans" ledger of humanity—but I still cling, by the edges of my fingernails, of not quite yet being a motherless child.

But the loss of a loved one? A mate? That's different. That's quantitatively different, because there is a factor involved that simply isn't there in a "generational", family, loss.

That factor is choice.

Your family—the generations that made you—loved you because you were part of them. You loved them because you were born to them, handed to them, imprinted on them since your first waking hour on this world. This was Mother. This was Father. These were Grandparents. You loved them and they loved you (other than in singularly unfortunate families, and mine was not one of those…) simply because it was already written in all of your DNA. There was nothing else to do but love—all of you belonged, you were part of the whole picture, you were the family, love was just part of that gestalt.

And then you grow up, and you look around at all the humanity teeming around you and who are strangers to you, and somehow one of those strangers looks back at you and a connection is made. There is nothing here that is written in the genes—nobody HAS to love you because you're you and they're themselves and love is written into that relationship—all of a sudden, love is a choice, a choice made freely, between two people who came from two different worlds one moment and belonged in a single shared world the next. There are of course entire books to be written about the kinds of these relationships too and naturally there are no guarantees at all and so many of these pairings are entered into for the wrong reasons or at the wrong time or they just don't 'take' properly and then you have breakups and divorces and acrimony… but there are those relationships which seem to exist so that one day you would grow up and become part of them. And if you are lucky enough to find one of those you are lucky indeed.

Except when it ends. When one of you is taken out of that picture.

"The death of a beloved is an amputation," C S Lewis writes in *A Grief Observed*. And he is right. It's the Phantom Mate syndrome, much like that of the Phantom Limb which you may have heard of in other contexts—the amputated leg or arm which still hurts, or itches, or moves, in your head as though it were still there and still attached. Your brain refuses to let go of its absence and simply assumes that something else must be in play—because how could that missing limb NOT be there? It was part of you. How could it just vanish away?

That's the kind of hole that a beloved leaves when they go. The place where you used to share dreams, meals, conversations, experiences. That empty place, which still hurts, still itches, the place where you expect to find them every time you turn around chasing the ghost of their shadow which you thought you just saw drifting by.

You chose, and you were chosen, and now the dance is ended, and the choice is evaporating, evanescent, a vapour of love. There's a piece that's missing out of your life, as though you were building a jigsaw puzzle and you find yourself nearly done but that last piece is gone, is missing, and there is a hole where it should have gone, and there is nothing at all you can do to fill that hole because the only piece that properly fit it is simply no longer in the same space-time continuum that you are and will never be again. And you're left sitting there staring at the forever incomplete puzzle, and there is nothing at all that you can do about it. Ever. Ever again. They're gone. If you're like me, or like C S Lewis, you might write about it, because that is what people like us do—it's a search for the memory of that piece, something we can put into that empty space even if just as a place holder. But, as he says in his own book, "Aren't all these notes the senseless writings of a man who won't accept the fact that there is nothing we can do with suffering except to suffer it?"

Perhaps I am just sensitized to things like this these days, but an essay by Rebecca Solnit which I tripped over on the Internet starts out with, "Moths drink the tears of sleeping birds."

Apparently there was an actual scientific report dated 2006 with that actual title, and Solnit's thoughts on the matter opened deep cracks in me. There is a giver and a taker here, one who sleeps and one who is awake and feeding on the dreams of the sleeper distilled into their night tears. There are apparently even accounts, from twenty years or more ago, of species of moth that would feed at the eyes of human beings (as documented by what must have been an appallingly dedicated entomologist by the name of Hans Bänziger, who allowed those moths to feed at his own…) There's even a word for the kind of sustenance practiced by the teardrinkers—"lacrhyphagous". I might have fed multitudes of them, legions of them, in this past year, and if I were any kind of artist I could draw them for you, this image of a woman looking up wide-eyed with her eyes pools of tears rimmed by moths lachryphaging at the fountainhead and growing richly coloured and fat and vivid on the nourishment of tears and of the sorrow that is dissolved in them. Solnit has a question at the end of her essay— "And this book, is it tears? Who drinks your tears… who hears your story?"

I weep words because that is what I know how to do.

If you are here, Reader, if you are holding this and reading this, if you understand any of it… then all I can say is, I welcome you gently into this vale of sorrow, although I so badly don't want to have to do it, and I can't possibly tell you how far you have to go. But it's a long road. And it's a lonely one. Perhaps it matters if only a little to know that you aren't alone. If you are here and you still have someone you love doing something in the next room… do me a favour. Go to them. Hug them. Tell them you love them. One of you is going to step into that eternity first—there will come a day when you won't be able to do that, or they will not. Never waste an opportunity to do it while you still can.

There will still be a hole left in the puzzle in the end, when all is said and done. Forever, you will find, is always shorter than you expected it to be. Forever is shorter than you expect… shorter than it used to be. Your forever is measured in the years that you get to share with the one you love. It is measurable. But it is all you have. All you will ever have. That, and the memories.

I asked my husband, while he was sitting in his hospital bed, a question which he misinterpreted somehow—he thought I was asking about his favourite movie, and after a brief consideration he said he didn't know but he thought "Love, Actually" might come close. And that fit—that the thing he treasured most… was love.

In one of the interlocking love stories from that movie, a young man brimming with unrequited and unrequitable love for the wife of his own best friend, basically tells her about it while also renouncing any intent of pursuing any of it, of wrecking her happiness to fulfill his own. And then he walks away from her, and whispers to himself, "Enough. Enough, now."

But the love remains. It always remains.

As I am writing these words in is November again, soon it will be a year that he left home for the last time never to return, and the first anniversary of his passing is almost upon me. I am numb with the expectation of that monster of sharp whirling blades which is about to descend upon me and cut my soul until it bleeds. But right now—in a moment of peace that comes before that storm, I am standing here with my eyes closed over the tears brimming from underneath, and whispering, enough, now. And remembering another movie—"Truly Madly Deeply"—in which a poem is quoted—one by Pablo Neruda (originally "La Muerta"):

No, forgive me.
If you are not living,
if you, beloved, my love,
if you
have died,

all the leaves will fall on my breast,
it will rain upon my soul night and day,
the snow will burn my heart,
I shall walk with cold and fire and death and snow,
my feet will want to march toward where you sleep, but
I shall go on living

Bewildered, bereft, abandoned, alone, aching… oh, my love. I am still living.

Acknowledgments

THIS WAS A BOOK WHICH was going to happen in any event – but I, somewhat optimistically, perhaps, chose to crowdfund it via Kickstarter. Somewhat to my astonishment it not only funded completely but even went a little over. There are a number of people who supported the campaign who were Deck's friends, and who did so out of a loving memory – but there were others, who barely knew him or only knew of grief and not of this particular loss, who also stepped up, and to all of them, I am grateful:

Jessica Conner, Tim Dunn-The Origami Guy, Scott Schaper, Ty Larson, Tracy Di Marco White, Cheryl L Martin, David Goldfarb, Lynnia, Rada, Meg Rose, Tobias S Buckell, Michelle Brenner, The Táhirih Project, John Martalo, M J Holt, deirdrebeth, NYC Coopers, Stef Maruch, Tina Anderson, Steve Pritchard, Pat MacEwen, Stan Field, Eldon Philips, Alex Jay Berman, Leigh Grossman, A. Parker Adams, Al Katerinsky, Randee Dawn, Liza Cameron Wasser, Laura Graf, Anthony R. Cardno, Jim and Ivy, Michele Eason-Priest, Robert Tienken, Matthew Mole, Mary K Collins, Brooks Moses, Steve Walter and others (some of whom did not wish to be thanked by name, and I respect that, but my gratitude is nonetheless great and no lesser than if their name appeared on this list.

Some supporters chose to do so because they too had lost those whom they loved, and knew this grief from the inside. It is therefore only just to mention these names as well, because they are mourned, and loved, and also gone.

In Memoriam
Dylan A Kowalewski, Robert Charles Mole, Dustin J

Gross, Denise Kennedy, Paul Silverstein, Aahz Maruch, Stephen Priest

I should also thank all the people who helped with the initial stages of getting a very raw manuscript into any kind of shape for publication – Paul Piper, Phyl Radford, Maya Kaathryn Bohnhof, Linda Karasti Beek, and other beta readers who pointed out places where grief overrode grammar or structure or found better images for that wonderful cover than I was capable of at the time.

Above all I should thank the friends who helped me survive the first year of widowhood, and who are still there for me, in particular Tim and Stacy Dunn, Mir Plemmons, and Deck's son David, and the folks at the Facebook group which gave me the space and the permission to mourn.

And, of course, there's the memory of the man about whom the entire book is, whose loss is so terribly difficult to bear, whom I possibly miss (if that is at all logically possible) even more now than I did in the first days of his passing. He has left a huge hole in my world, one which I will quite possibly never fill again because there isn't another like him in this world. Like I said to him, in the note I sent up to the sky where I left him, if I don't see you again here, love, I will find you in that place where no shadows fall. Someday we will meet again.

Alma Alexander

About the Author

ALMA ALEXANDER'S LIFE SO FAR has prepared her very well for her chosen career. She was born in a country which no longer exists on the maps, has lived and worked in seven countries on four continents (and in cyberspace!), has climbed mountains, dived in coral reefs, flown small planes, swum with dolphins, touched two-thousand-year-old tiles in a gate out of Babylon. She is a novelist, anthologist and short story writer who currently shares her life between the Pacific Northwest of the USA (where she lives with two obligatory writer's cats) and the wonderful fantasy worlds of her own imagination.

You can find out more about Alma and her books on:

Her website (www.AlmaAlexander.org)

Amazon author page (https://amzn.to/2N6xE9u)

Twitter (https://twitter.com/AlmaAlexander)

Facebook page (https://www.facebook.com/AuthorAlmaAlexander/)

Patreon (https://www.patreon.com/AlmaAlexander)

About Book View Café

Book View Café is a professional authors' cooperative offering high-quality DRM-free ebooks in multiple formats to readers around the world. With authors in a variety of genres including mystery, romance, fantasy, and science fiction, Book View Café has something for everyone. 90% of the profits from the sales of BVC books goes directly to the authors.

Book View Café authors (past and present) include Nebula, Hugo, Endeavour, and Philip K. Dick Award winners – Nebula, Hugo, World Fantasy, Rita Award and regional State Book Award nominees and finalists – as well as New York Times bestsellers and notable book authors.

http://bookviewcafe.com

Other books by Alma Alexander available from Book View Café

Abducticon

Empress

Val Hall: The Even Years
Val Hall: The Odd Years

Fractured Fairy Tales

Wings of Fire

Changer of Days: 20th Anniversary Edition

The Were Chronicles Omnibus (Random, Wolf, Shifter)